Le

New Directions in Philosophy and Cognitive Science

Series Editor: **John Protevi, Louisiana State University**

This series brings together work that takes cognitive science in new directions. Hitherto, philosophical reflection on cognitive science – or perhaps better, philosophical contribution to the interdisciplinary field that is cognitive science – has for the most part come from philosophers with a commitment to a representationalist model of the mind.

However, as cognitive science continues to make advances, especially in its neuroscience and robotics aspects, there is growing discontent with the representationalism of traditional philosophical interpretations of cognition. Cognitive scientists and philosophers have turned to a variety of sources – phenomenology and dynamic systems theory foremost among them to date – to rethink cognition as the direction of the action of an embodied and affectively attuned organism embedded in its social world, a stance that sees representation as only one tool of cognition, and a derived one at that.

To foster this growing interest in rethinking traditional philosophical notions of cognition – using phenomenology, dynamic systems theory, and perhaps other approaches yet to be identified – we dedicate this series to "New Directions in Philosophy and Cognitive Science."

Titles include:

Richard Menary
COGNITIVE INTEGRATION
Mind and Cognition Unbounded

New Directions in Philosophy and Cognitive Science
Series Standing Order ISBN 978–0–230–54935–7 Hardback
978–0–230–54936–4 Paperback
(*outside North America only*)

You can receive future titles in this series as they are published by placing a standing order. Please contact your bookseller or, in case of difficulty, write to us at the address below with your name and address, the title of the series and the ISBN quoted above.

Customer Services Department, Macmillan Distribution Ltd, Houndmills, Basingstoke, Hampshire RG21 6XS, England

Also by Richard Menary

RADICAL ENACTIVISM (*editor*)
THE EXTENDED MIND (*editor*)

Cognitive Integration
Mind and Cognition Unbounded

Richard Menary
University of Wollongong

palgrave
macmillan

First published 2007 by
PALGRAVE MACMILLAN
Houndmills, Basingstoke, Hampshire RG21 6XS and
175 Fifth Avenue, New York, N.Y. 10010
Companies and representatives throughout the world

PALGRAVE MACMILLAN is the global academic imprint of the Palgrave Macmillan division of St. Martin's Press, LLC and of Palgrave Macmillan Ltd. Macmillan® is a registered trademark in the United States, United Kingdom and other countries. Palgrave is a registered trademark in the European Union and other countries.

ISBN-13: 978–1–4039–8977–2 hardback
ISBN-10: 1–4039–8977–X hardback

This book is printed on paper suitable for recycling and made from fully managed and sustained forest sources. Logging, pulping and manufacturing processes are expected to conform to the environmental regulations of the country of origin.

A catalogue record for this book is available from the British Library.

A catalog record for this book is available from the Library of Congress.

10   9   8   7   6   5   4   3   2
16   15   14   13   12   11   10   09   08

Printed and bound in Great Britain by
CPI Antony Rowe, Chippenham and Eastbourne

For Sarah with love and admiration

Contents

Acknowledgements

Thanks to Andy Clark, John Sutton, David Papineau, Mike Wheeler, Mark Rowlands, Shaun Gallagher, Dan Hutto, Dan Fitzpatrick, Matthew Ratcliffe and Stephen Cowley for various conversations that helped shape my ideas. Thanks also to my MA students during 2006–7 where some of the material from the book was presented and discussed, especially Laura Mundy and Joanna Gillies. Thanks especially to Andy Clark and John Sutton, who both read through and commented on an early draft of the book. Special thanks must go to Dan Bunyard, whose editorial support and patience has been very gratefully received.

Thanks to my parents for setting me on the right path and for their unwavering support of my intellectual endeavours, they have been an inspiration to me. Thanks especially to my wife Sarah, who has kept my sometimes flagging spirits high and who provided practical as well as emotional support.

Chapter 3 reproduces material published as "Attacking the Bounds of Cognition," which appeared in *Philosophical Psychology*, Vol. 19, No. 3, June © 2006, pp. 329–344.

Foreword

We are very happy to inaugurate the series New Directions in Philosophy and Cognitive Science with Richard Menary's *Cognitive Integration: Mind and Cognition Unbounded*. Menary undertakes the definition and defense of "cognitive integration" as an updating and refinement of theses on what we can call 4E cognition: embodied, embedded, extended and enactive cognition. Using research in dynamic systems theory, bodily schemas, and social practice, Menary explains how neural and bodily functions are integrated with each other and with the manipulation of linguistic and other extra-bodily representational vehicles in pursuit of cognitive goals in normatively governed practices.

Menary's approach enables him to engage internalist and individualist critics of 4E cognition as well as to differentiate his account from other forms of work in 4E cognition. In doing so, he clears the ground for his own positive account, which he develops in terms of four theses: the manipulation thesis, the hybrid mind thesis, the cognitive practices thesis and the transformation thesis. Covering research in evolution, linguistics, semiotics, developmental psychology and other fields, Menary's work stakes out a nuanced yet clearly stated position at the forefront of some of the most interesting work in cognitive science and philosophy of mind, taking it in new directions.

Introduction

"What do you think about spiders and their webs?" is not a question you are likely to be asked very often. You *might* answer, "very pretty, on a crisp November morning with the dew hanging delicately like tiny silver bells from the thin elegant strands." The answer I am looking for does not concern those aesthetic qualities, it concerns what you think the relation between the spider and her web is. Do you think that the web is simply a product of the relevant organs of the spider, albeit a product crucial to its ability to catch prey? Or do you think that the web is a part of the spider's prey-catching system – a system that is not bounded by the body of the spider but includes the web? After all, the spider creates and carefully maintains and manipulates the web and it is through the web that she is able to efficiently catch and consume her prey. If you are inclined to think that the organism is bounded by its body and that, therefore, the web is not really a part of the organismic system because it is not part of the body, then it is my purpose to persuade you that there may not be any very good reasons for thinking this.

For example, Dawkins argues that "in a very real sense her web is a temporary functional extension of her body, a huge extension of the effective catchment area of her predatory organs" (Dawkins 1982, p. 198). In response you might offer the view that an organism is bounded by its body because it is an obvious and observable spatial boundary. However, biology goes beyond this seemingly obvious conclusion that might be reached at first glance. Biologists and philosophers of Biology are telling us that the organismic system is one that is not limited by the spatial bounds of the body.

To be able to understand the organismic system, as Millikan puts it, as not simply bounded by the body, one has to understand the organism's place in and relation to its environment. The spider's ability to catch prey is an organismic process, and one must analyse the co-ordination of the functioning of the parts of the spider, including the web, in concert. This is important, for web and predatory, perceptual and motor organs each have a role to play in this process and these roles must be co-ordinated.

Millikan takes the co-ordination of subsystems to be the definition of an organismic system, involving... "a co-ordination among parts or subsystems, each of which requires that the other parts or subsystems have normal structure and are functioning normally" (Millikan 1993, p. 160). In this way, Millikan argues against identifying the organismic system in terms of a spatial bodily boundary, such that parts of the system are spatially internal and the environment is spatially external. Far from it, for the purposes of understanding the spider's ability to catch prey, we must analyse the organismic system in terms of the co-ordination between subsystems of the spider including the web.

What I think about the relation between a spider and its web is closer to Millikan than Dawkins, because, although I agree with Dawkins that the phenotype is not bounded by the body, the spider's web is not simply a temporary extension of the spider's predatory organs. The spider has a long-standing capacity to create, maintain and manipulate its webs. The integration of the spider's predatory organs with the spider's web allows the spider to do something in a way it would otherwise find it very difficult to do – that is, catch prey. Furthermore, the ability of the spider not only to create webs, but also to maintain and manipulate them is an adaptation of the spider; the spider and its web are under selective pressure. To understand how the spider catches its prey, we need to explain how it manipulates the web, for example how she senses vibrations in the strands caused by a struggling fly. As such, it is the co-ordination of spider and web that is the unit of interest.

This is mirrored in the issue about whether cognition and thinking has a spatial boundary. A popular position is to think of cognitive systems as systems of the brain. In philosophy this usually goes hand in hand with a commitment to some form of mind – brain supervenience; if so then cognition has a natural boundary, it is contained by the brain. It follows that if you want to study cognition and the mind, then you need to study the systems responsible for cognitive and mental phenomena implemented in the brain. Furthermore, it may be that we believe that the "bounded by the brain" view is quite common-sensical, the mind is indeed "in the head". In what sense, then, are cognitive systems and cognitive processes more like the case of the spider and her web?

One clear sense is the long-standing capacity of Humans to create linguistic and representational surrounds and then to maintain and manipulate them. The exercising of this capacity is of course fleeting, although the long-standing disposition is not. We often, for example, write out mathematical problems, rather than completing them "in the head". Another sense is the direct manipulation of the environment to complete cognitive tasks. For example, expert players of the game Tetris prefer to rotate the shapes on the screen using buttons, rather than by rotating images of them "in the head". If cognition is bounded by the brain, why do we not complete all these cognitive tasks, and many others like them, "in the head?"

Cognitive integration provides an answer to this question. Its cash value is that the co-ordination of bodily processes of the organism with salient features of the environment, often created or maintained by the organism, allows it to perform cognitive functions that it otherwise would be unable to; or allows it to perform functions in a way that is distinctively different and is an improvement upon the way that the organism performs those functions via bodily processes alone.

The brain, of course, plays a central role in this wider systemic process. It is, in a sense, an organ for completing cognitive tasks; it does much else besides, of course. Cognitive scientists have attempted to model the systems and processes of the brain by which it is able to complete cognitive tasks. Sometimes these models are at a high level of abstraction, sometimes they take into account actual neurological details. In terms of laboratory tasks these models often have explanatory goodness, but there is a question mark over their ecological validity (Neisser 1976, 1981). Just as it would be folly for the evolutionary biologist to focus exclusively upon the bodily organs of the spider and not upon the co-ordination of bodily organs with web, those concerned with ecological validity in the cognitive case think it folly to focus exclusively on the brain and not on the co-ordination of brain, body and local environment.

The position that I will develop in this book is that cognition does not have a spatial boundary that lies at the periphery of the brain, or even at the skin. As Millikan succinctly puts it, "I no more carry my complete cognitive systems around with me as I walk from place to place than I carry the U.S. currency system about with me when I walk with a dime in my pocket" (Millikan 1993, p. 170).

The aim of this book is to explain what it means for cognition not to be bounded by the brain. Cognitive systems function through the integration of neural functions, bodily functions and the functions of linguistic and other representational vehicles. The appeal to integration is cashed out in terms of the co-ordination of these functions.

Developing the integrationist position begins with the fact of our embodiment. But what does this fact tell us, if anything, about our cognitive and mental lives? Embodied approaches to the mind and cognition are supposed to reveal to us something profound about the *embodiedness* of our minds that we ought to understand the mind as *shaped* by the body. However, there seems to be a bifurcation of approach in the embodied mind community. There is on the one hand the phenomenologically inspired approach of Gallagher (2005) with a detailed account of how bodily activity in the environment constrains what we perceive and of what we are consciously aware. This approach takes seriously the detailed description of embodiment with regard to cognitive and mental capacities such as perception and social cognition. Then there is the distributed/extended approach to cognition and mind of the likes of Hutchins (1995), Clark (1997, 2003) and Rowlands (1999), who begin with the assumption that cognition is embodied but then concentrate on the ways in which we interact, bodily, with the environment. They take seriously detailed descriptions of manipulations of external representational vehicles such as diagrams, mathematical notations or written sentences with regard to mental and cognitive capacities such as memory and belief. Distributed cognition does not give a detailed account of the way in which the body shapes cognition in these cases, rather they tend to focus on how external vehicles (artefacts, representations) shape and transform cognitive capacities.

The difference in approach does not constitute a profound difference. Rather, we are approaching the same phenomenon from different directions. Therefore, we need to reconceive the mind on both bodily and environmental grounds. For example, integrationists take the manipulation of external vehicles to be a pre-requisite for higher cognition and that embodied engagement is a pre-condition for these manipulative abilities. Therefore, it would be a mistake not only to disengage the body from its environment, but also to ignore the contribution of external representational systems to our cognitive capacities. A straightforward way of understanding the position of cognitive integration is in terms of bodily engagement with vehicles in the extra-bodily environment, in such a way that they are integrated into a whole.

However, the two approaches have not been adequately brought into relation with one another. I seek to do this by uniting them in the integrationist position. Most work has been aimed at the dynamics of integrated systems, focusing on the bio-causal co-ordinations between bodily and extra-bodily parts of the system – usually referred to in the literature as reciprocal coupling (Clark 1997, Hurley 1998, Wheeler 2005). Whilst at the same time there have been discussions of the types of representational vehicle that are manipulated during the bio-causal co-ordinations (Clark and Chalmers 1998, Rowlands 1999, Clark 2006).

These theorists maintain that the study of bio-cultural representational systems is reliant upon a clear understanding of those systems as structured by bio-causal co-ordinations and that the functioning of the system requires the stability and availability of extra-bodily vehicles and the bodily manipulation of those vehicles. This is certainly true, but these explanatory projects lack the resources to fully explain how and why we manipulate extra-bodily vehicles in the way that we do. To do this satisfactorily we need to place the dynamics of the system in a wider cultural and normative setting. Our abilities to manipulate the extra-bodily environment are normative and are largely dependent upon our learning and training histories. Hence, explanations of the dynamics of integrated cognitive systems will only be one, important, explanatory factor.

Within the wider setting, manipulations of representations are embedded in a practice, which has a normative as well as a physical/causal dimension, such as the practice of manipulating mathematical notations. The practice of manipulating a representation is normative because we learn how to manipulate the representations correctly and because of the cognitive purpose of the practice. The purpose is to achieve a particular kind of goal, such as solving a problem, planning or making inferences which I call the cognitive task. It follows that we will need a developmental account of how we learn cognitive practices.

There are three complementary ways in which we can understand integration:

1. Reciprocal Causation/Bio-causal Co-ordinations: The dynamical approach analyses the reciprocal coupling between systems which are part of a larger system. They have causal influence over each other for as long as they are coupled. This is a symmetrical relation, the two systems are mutually constraining of each other's behaviour.
2. Embodied Engagement: The body is integrated with the environment through its body schemas, which are unconscious sensorimotor programmes for action. These programmes often integrate with the environment in two ways, first by training (or evolutionary adaptation) and secondly by norms-governing practices such as driving, playing a sport such as tennis and writing.
3. The Manipulation Thesis: Humans manipulate their local environment with their bodies. They might directly manipulate the physical structure of the environment and they might use tools to do this. They create artefacts, such as tools and representational vehicles. Humans very often create and manipulate external representational vehicles to complete a cognitive task. In doing so, they are carrying out a cognitive practice which is governed by its own norms, which I call cognitive norms.

Just as the spider and its web are dynamically interacting parts of an organismic process (catching prey), the human and its external representational vehicles are dynamically interacting parts of a cognitive process. The spider integrates with its web through its body and we integrate with environmental vehicles through our bodies – there is no action at a distance here. The spider is disposed to create and manipulate the web in various ways that facilitate the catching of prey. Similarly we bodily integrate with, create and manipulate external vehicles in various ways that facilitate the completion of cognitive tasks.

If we studied the spider's ability to catch prey without taking account of its web, we would not have much of an explanation at all.

If we were to take away the spider's ability to create and manipulate its webs, we would severely curtail its ability to catch prey. Similarly, I suggest, studying the cognitive abilities of the human organism without taking account of its bodily manipulations of environmental vehicles is not much of an explanation at all, and if we were to take away the human organism's abilities to bodily manipulate its environment we would severely curtail its cognitive abilities.

Cognitive integration is an explanatory framework that is incompatible with psychological and neural internalists and individualists, who try to explain our cognitive abilities by denying the explanatory relevance of the environment and our bodily engagements with it.

The book is structured in two parts, the first sets the scene for cognitive integration. In Chapter 1, I survey some of the reasons for being an internalist that stem from cognitivism, the view that cognition is the processing of representations and certain influential metaphysical assumptions. The first of these is that the only genuinely causal capacities are ones that supervene on intrinsic properties. In the psychological case, cognitive capacities supervene on intrinsic neural properties of the individual. Arguments for cognitive internalism which rely upon these metaphysical assumptions are not very successful.

In Chapter 2, I outline the dynamical approach that gives us the notion of reciprocal coupling – a symmetrical causal relation – and then differentiate it from asymmetric forms of externalism. I then turn to active externalism and the extended mind, which makes use of the dynamical notion of reciprocal coupling. However, I suggest that there is a problem with parity-based formulations of the extended mind which leave it open to internalist objections. Although the extended mind framework does make use of the notion of reciprocal coupling, it does not include the normative account of bodily manipulations of external vehicles. This is a big difference between the extended mind and cognitive integration. In Chapter 3, I show how the internalist objections to the extended mind framework can be dealt with by the integrational framework. The first three chapters constitute the first part of the book.

The second part of the book concerns the formulation of cognitive integration in terms of four theses: the manipulation thesis, the hybrid mind thesis, the cognitive practices thesis and the transformation thesis. Chapter 4 concerns the manipulation thesis. Rather than focusing on the manipulation thesis as a matter of location and constitution, I focus on manipulation as an embodied engagement with the local environment, which is governed by norms. I then go on to classify bodily manipulations by class and I identify four general classes:

- *Biological Coupling*: such as extended phenotypes (Dawkins 1982), animate vision (Ballard 1991) and SMC (O'Reagan and Noe 2001).
- *Epistemic Actions*: using the environment as its own representation, obviating the need for endogenous representations – as in Tetris (Kirsh and Maglio 1994).
- *Self–Correcting Actions*: the use of language and external props to direct and structure practical actions in completing tasks.
- *Cognitive Practices*: the manipulation of exogenous representational and notational systems according to certain normative practices – as in mathematics (Vygotsky 1978, Karmiloff-Smith 1992, Menary 2006a).

I provide examples of the first two classes and then an analysis of representations (called the Peircean principle) that does not presuppose that they are internal or external, as preparation for the next two chapters.

Chapter 5 looks at the biological basis for cognitive integration, developing themes introduced at the beginning of this introduction. The manipulation thesis and the Peircean principle feed into the hybrid mind thesis, that cognitive and mental processes are hybrids of internal and bodily external manipulations of vehicles. This thesis has a biological basis in extended phenotypes and organism – environment transactions generally. Bodily manipulations of the environment are adaptations – giving manipulative abilities a phylogenetic history – but the manipulative abilities are often fine-tuned by the environment in ontogeny – in the human case through learning and training. Thus, there is a continuity between the classes of manipulation from the biological cases right up to cognitive practices which involve normative fine-tuning of the body schemas that underlie our manipulative abilities.

In Chapter 6, I turn to cognitive practices. The normative nature of integrated cognitive capacities is best illustrated by the class of manipulations I dub cognitive practices. I outline the cognitive norms by which external representations are manipulated, then I examine the variety of forms of representation and the cognitive ends to which they are put. I then put the notions to work by giving an integrational account of our systematic linguistic capacities. Rather than give an internalist explanation of these abilities, by positing a language of thought, I show that systematicity is dependent upon our being able to recognise grammatical forms and pragmatic and semantic constraints on public language. An internalist explanation that relies only upon syntactic features of internal tokens of the language of thought is inadequate because it does not have access to grammatical forms of natural language and pragmatic and semantic constraints. I then begin to develop the account further by indicating that these abilities are fostered by exposure to public language in learning and training situations. Linguistic systematicity is, therefore, just a version of our general ability to manipulate external vehicles of public language.

This leads us directly to an account of the transformation of our manipulative abilities in ontogeny by training and learning. A Vygotskian framework is provided for this and the chapter concludes with an account of the kind of training required for systematic linguistic abilities.

1
Cognitivism and Internalism

Modern philosophy has never been able to quite shake off
the Cartesian idea of the mind, as something that "resides," –
such is the term, – in the pineal gland. Everybody laughs
at this nowadays, and yet everybody continues to think of
mind in this same general way, as something within this
person or that, belonging to him and correlative to the
real world.

– Charles Sanders Peirce

1.1 Introduction

Cognitivism represents the major shift in the study of cognition
after behaviourism and underpins the main theories and methodolo-
gies of cognitive science. In contrast to behaviourism, which focuses
on observable behaviour, cognitivism posits internal representations.
The explanatory focus turns to the processing of these representations to explain cognitive phenomena such as memory and is also
used to explain observable behaviour. Cognition is simply defined as
the processing of representations.

This claim is usually coupled to an assumption about where the
representations are located and I will call this assumption "cognitive
internalism." The assumption amounts to this: cognitive processes,
whether computational or otherwise, occur inside the head. Hence,
we find that cognitive processes and representations are "internal"
and that they do not depend upon anything "external" to the
cogniser. In other words, cognitive vehicles and processes are

individuated independently of what goes on in the "external environment" of the cogniser – except perhaps for their content. A methodological moral follows: the study of cognitive processes should appeal only to what is inside the head. The point of this chapter is to show that cognitivism does not have to be an internalist doctrine. It is quite consistent with cognitive integration, which allows that some manipulations of external representational vehicles are cognitive processes. The internalist version of cognitivism is based upon some dubious metaphysical assumptions which nobody has quite been able to shake philosophers out of.[1] The direction of argument is simple; cognitivism is consistent with integration despite certain cherished assumptions about causal capacities and computational systems.

I will consider two arguments in favour of internalism that display the background metaphysical assumptions in question: Fodor's (1987) argument from causal capacities and, what I shall call, the computational argument (Fodor 1980, Segal 1989, Egan 1992). The causal capacities argument runs like this: (1) Science taxonomises by causal capacities (what an entity can cause). (2) The causal capacities an entity has supervened upon its intrinsic causal properties. (3) In the psychological case, the causal properties supervene upon local neural structure. (4) Therefore, cognitive capacities supervene upon intrinsic properties of the individual. Looked at in this way, the argument is a defence of mind–brain supervenience and I shall take it to be an argument in favour of cognitive vehicles and processes being located in the head. The argument is unsound if premises 2 and 3 are false. There are plenty of examples across the sciences that show premise 2 to be false. Cognitive integrationists think that premise 3 is false. The argument is important because it depends upon several metaphysical assumptions which drive an internalist reading of cognitivism. The primary metaphysical assumption is that only intrinsic physical properties are truly causal, they are the only properties that figure in genuinely causal generalisations. This assumption just turns out to be false in many of the sciences, including biology and the social sciences. Contemporary counter-arguments to cognitive integration (Adams and Aizawa 2001, 2007, Rupert 2004, 2007) depend upon this assumption in their appeal against genuine causal generalisations in psychology that involve anything other than intrinsic properties of the individual.

Wilson (1995, p. 64) gives us a version of the computational argument: (A) The sciences of cognition taxonomically individuate mental processes only qua computational processes. (B) The computational states and processes that an individual instantiates supervene on the intrinsic states of that individual. Therefore, (C) The sciences of cognition individuate states and processes that supervene on the intrinsic physical states of the individual who instantiates those states and processes. I will take the computational argument to be an argument in favour of the individuative independence of cognitive vehicles from the external environment. This argument is unsound if premise B is false. Clearly, premise A is false if not all cognitive processes are computational. Premise B is false if some cognitive processes are not intrinsic. I will not directly be arguing against A, I will be arguing for the conclusion that cognitive processes and vehicles are not intrinsic in the individualist sense.

The computational argument is important because the idea that a natural (or wide) psychology would be too difficult is a direct ancestor of Adams and Aizawa's complaint that such a science would amount to a disconnected motley (this complaint will be dealt with in Chapter 3).

Before turning to these arguments, I outline some of the terminology that will be retained from cognitivism, because cognitive integration is quite compatible with cognitivism once the internalist assumption has been removed from it.

1.2   What is a cognitive process and what is a cognitive system?

Most philosophers and cognitive scientists take cognition to be a clump of mental acts or processes that come under broad headings such as remembering, perceiving, learning and reasoning. Identifying what makes a process cognitive is more difficult. In a recent paper critical of the extended mind, processes that exhibit the mark of the cognitive are identified as those that involve representations with non-derived [intrinsic] content (Adams and Aizawa 2001). However, it is not only notoriously difficult to specify just what intrinsic content is supposed to be (Hutto 1999, Dennett 1990, Mendola 2003), but also the definition looks to be unduly restrictive (I shall have more to say about this condition in Chapter 4). Furthermore, we do not find cognitive scientists providing definitions of the "mark of the cognitive" as a preliminary to their empirical investigations.[2]

In general, there is no real agreement in the cognitive science community upon a definition of what a cognitive process is, nor of the vehicles of cognition. Or, we could look at the situation a different way, cognitive scientists are pluralistic about the kinds of things they count as cognitive processes and vehicles. For example, classical computationalists take the vehicles of cognition to be symbols that have formal, or syntactic, properties in virtue of which they are processed (Fodor and Pylyshyn 1988). Connectionist vehicles of cognition are not symbolic; instead they are patterns of activation distributed across nodes in a network. Connectionists understand cognitive processes to be algorithms for the spread of activation across the network (Smolensky 1988, 1995).

It is quite natural to be pluralistic about cognitive processes and vehicles; as such, there is no single genuine "cognitive kind".[3] In general, we might specify that a cognitive process is one that involves the manipulation of a cognitive vehicle in the completion of a cognitive task. The classical–connectionist debate demonstrates that there is a plurality of types of manipulations and vehicles. Furthermore, it may be the case that not all cognitive vehicles are representational vehicles. Take, for example, the role of the ambient array in ecological theories of perception (Gibson 1979).

We do have a sense of the cognitive task, to which the notion of cognitive process is surely central. Rowlands gives us a general sense of the cognitive task (2003, p. 161):

> it does seem fairly clear that the notion of a cognitive process is defined, in part, in terms of the notion of a cognitive task. A cognitive process is one that plays a fairly central role in allowing a subject to accomplish a cognitive task.

Quite generally, cognitive tasks are ones such as perceiving the world, remembering things about the world and employing things remembered in making inferences, problem solving and the like (Rowlands 2003). However, a general definition of a cognitive task can easily end up being unhelpfully vacuous. If we define the cognitive task as any task for the completion of which cognition is required, then almost every task will be a cognitive one. I think it is more helpful if we think of cognitive tasks as involving the exercise of particular cognitive capacities such as remembering a date, solving a problem, learning to do something and so on. These are tasks where the exercising of cognitive capacities is directly tied to their successful completion.

Perhaps there is more clarity about the notion of a cognitive system? There are two senses of cognitive system, which we need to distinguish. That of a particular cognitive system – for example the memory system as it might be – and the overall system, of which these specialised sub-systems are parts. However, there is not even agreement on what a cognitive system is in either of these senses. One very general way of thinking about cognitive systems is that they are the mechanisms that underlie the processes involved in remembering, perceiving, learning and reasoning and so on. A theory of cognitive architecture, such as classicism or connectionism, is supposed to specify the nature of these mechanisms. Classicists and connectionists have generally agreed that the mechanisms that underlie cognitive processes are all in the cranium; they endorse the assumption of cognitive internalism. I turn now to look in a bit more detail at the classical and non-classical visions of cognition.

1.3 The classical and non-classical visions

As mentioned in the previous section, cognitive processes and vehicles in cognitive science are understood in both a classical and a connectionist way. Classically cognition has been understood as the processing of representational vehicles. Representations are intentional entities, in that they are directed at something else, this is what it is for them to mean something, or have content. They are complex, in that they can have constituent parts, linguistic representations being a case in point. Call these classical vehicles.

However, not all cognition involves manipulations of vehicles as classically conceived. Neural networks, animate (Ballard 1991), ecological (Gibson 1979) and sensorimotor (O'Regan and Noë 2001) accounts of perception do not involve manipulations of classical vehicles. In neural networks, there are patterns of activation distributed across aggregates of neurons and in ecological theories of perception there are perceptual mechanisms which are directed at environmental variables that afford action. We can identify the directedness of the patterns of activation as well as mechanisms and their affordances, such that they at least have an intentional aspect. What they do not have are the articulate and complexly structured contents of classical vehicles. Call these non-classical vehicles.

So, there is a distinction between classical and non-classical vehicles of cognition and there will be differences in the way they are manipulated. I shall take manipulations of vehicles to be general enough to cover both classical and non-classical cases. I shall take the following definition of a cognitive process as standard throughout the book:

> *A process is cognitive when it aims at completing a cognitive task; and it is constituted by manipulating a vehicle.*

This is a very general definition which does not tie us to a process or vehicle having to be internal or external, or whether vehicles must be representations or have a particular kind of content. I take it to be a working definition rather than a set of necessary and sufficient conditions and I expect each case to be judged on its cognitive merits. I do not think, for example, that switching on a television with a remote control constitutes a cognitive process – care needs to be taken in formulating the cognitive task here.[4] More controversially, I do not think that tapping numbers into a calculator constitutes a cognitive process. Even though there is a clear sense – in which such a manipulation aims at completing a cognitive task – care needs to be taken in formulating the type of manipulation here.[5]

I do not think that internalists will very likely be persuaded by definitions anyway. However, I do think that a careful explanation of the manipulation thesis and types of manipulation in Chapters 5, 6 and 7, will prove more persuasive.

The integrationist takes cognition to be hybrid in that it is made up of classical and non-classical vehicles and processes and that some of these processes and vehicles will be bodily internal and others bodily external. I turn now to outlining the main claims of cognitive internalists (who often call themselves individualists), before moving on to the arguments.

1.4 Cognitive internalism

Cognitive internalists take the distinction between what is inside the head and what is outside of it to be significant. They argue that cognitive processes are located in the head and that consequently the study of cognition should make reference only to what goes on inside the head. Cognitive internalists often refer to themselves as psychological individualists (Stich 1983, Fodor 1987, Egan 1991, Segal 1991, Burge 1986). For example, Stich provides a constraint upon explanation and taxonomy in the cognitive and psychological sciences, which he calls the principle of autonomy:

> The basic idea of the principle is that the states and processes that ought to be of concern to the psychologist are those that supervene on the current, internal, physical state of the organism... Any differences between organisms which do not manifest themselves as differences in their *current, internal, physical* states ought to be ignored by a psychological theory. (1983, p. 164) [My italics]

Cognition is largely autonomous of what goes on outside the head, but integrationists argue that cognitive vehicles and processes are, at least, partly constituted by what goes on outside the head. The autonomy principle rules out the possibility of integrationist explanations in cognitive science.

Individualists often use a further methodological constraint, methodological solipsism (Fodor 1980). The psychological and cognitive sciences ought to taxonomise/individuate cognitive vehicles and processes only in terms of their formal properties – this is known as the formality condition. This is because cognitive processes are computational processes and only have access to the formal properties of cognitive states. We get solipsism because the cognitive states in question are taken to be *narrow*, they are states that do not presuppose anything about the external world of the individual who has them (Fodor 1980).

The Individualist has it that cognitive processes, and the cognitive vehicles which those processes apply to, are taxonomised as a kind in terms of their computational properties and causal capacities. If it can be independently shown that computational properties and causal capacities supervene only upon the internal, intrinsic, physical properties of an individual, such as his or her brain states, then internalism about cognitive vehicles and processes follows.

However, the formality condition does not tell us anything about the location of cognitive vehicles, they might well be external. Cognitive integrationists must argue against the claim that the formality condition requires cognitive vehicles to be individuated narrowly. Of course, if there are external cognitive vehicles, then it is clear that they will be given a wide individuation. As such, cognitive integrationists *need* have no quarrel with the formality condition, some cognitive processes may well turn out to be computational;[6] their argument is with the narrow individuation of cognitive vehicles and processes.

Michael Devitt (1990, p. 377) summarises the main claims of individualism:

1 Psychology explains why given certain stimuli at her sense organs, a person behaved in a certain way.
2 Only something that is entirely supervenient on what is inside her skin – on her intrinsic internal physical states, particularly her brain – could play the required explanatory role between peripheral input and output.
3 Environmental causes of her stimuli and effects of her behaviour are beside the psychological point.
4 Cognitive processes and cognitive vehicles must be individuated according to their role within the individual, without regard to their relations to an environment.

I shall now examine the argument from causal capacities and the computational argument, as arguments for the conclusion that cognitive kinds supervene on intrinsic properties of individuals.

1.5 The argument from causal capacities

Fodor puts forward his argument from causal capacities[7] in the second chapter of *Psychosemantics* (1987). A causal capacity is just the capacity to bring about, or cause, an effect. Whilst the argument is primarily designed to show that taxonomy (individuation of kinds) in psychology cannot be by wide content, it is in its own right an argument for cognitive internalism. We shall evaluate it as an argument for cognitive internalism, ignoring the ramifications for theories of content.

The argument really has two crucial steps, the first being that the sciences individuate causal capacities by specifying the relevant intrinsic causal properties a thing has. This claim is false because many sciences individuate by wide causal properties and Fodor himself acknowledges this. The scope of the claim is therefore wrong. Science sometimes individuates causal capacities by intrinsic properties and sometimes by wide[8] properties.

The second step is to insist that causal capacities are supervenient only upon intrinsic properties, because even if wide properties are sometimes used to individuate causal capacities they never themselves constitute causal capacities. This claim is again false across many of the sciences. It drives an intuitive reaction to cognitive integration: how could something bodily external to the organism be part of its causal capacity to do something? In response, I develop the notion of a wide capacity, which is akin to Wilson's wide realisation (Wilson 2004), where a capacity is realised by the organism as part of some wider system that extends beyond the bodily boundaries of the organism. I shall proceed by taking each of these two stages of the argument in turn.

1.5.1   Individuation by intrinsic causal properties

Fodor's first premise is that science taxonomises by causal capacities (what an entity can cause).

> We want science to give causal explanations of such things (events, whatever) in nature as can be causally explained. Giving such explanations essentially involves projecting and confirming causal generalizations. And causal generalizations subsume the things they apply to in virtue of the causal properties of the things that they apply to. Of course. (1987, p. 34)

To follow the argument we will have to go along with this premise and I shall not subject it to scrutiny here.

The second premise can be stated in either a weak or a strong form: the causal capacities an entity has supervene upon the causal properties it has; or the causal capacities an entity has supervene upon the *intrinsic* causal properties it has.

The issue here is simply whether wide properties can be counted as genuinely causal. If we use the weaker version then the possibility that they are is left open. The second option restricts the possibility to intrinsic properties alone. Fodor is inclined to lean towards the weaker version at times:

In short, what you need in order to do science is a taxonomic apparatus that distinguishes between things insofar as they have different causal properties, and that groups things together insofar as they have the same causal properties. (1987, p. 34)

Let us assume that Fodor is right about this; although some have disagreed,[9] how would we generate cognitive internalism from it? We can generate internalism by narrowing the explanation of a causal capacity to include only intrinsic properties, ignoring wide properties even where they may be relevant. Take the following simple example from the Churchlands:

A neuron cannot know the distant causal ancestry of its inputs and outputs. An activated neuron causes a creature to withdraw into its shell not because such activation represents the presence of a predator – though it may indeed represent this – but because that neuron is connected to the withdrawal muscles, and because its activation is of the kind that causes them to contract. (1983, p. 305)

Neuron A has the causal capacity to cause muscle contraction, because it has the causal property of spiking at a particular threshold, other causal properties which neuron A has will be irrelevant to this particular causal capacity. So, in the above case the historical property of neuron A – that it has been activated in the presence of a predator – is irrelevant to the causal capacity of muscle contraction. If we are considering how the organism has the capacity to retract muscles, then the causal properties in question will be intrinsic. However, if we want to explain how the creature has the capacity to withdraw into its shell in the presence of predators, then we will need an account of the activation of the neuron in the presence of predators and, therefore, make reference to its wide properties.

If the history of the organism and the environment it is located in are relevant to the explanation of the causal capacity of withdrawing into its shell in the presence of predators, then taxonomy is also by wide properties.

This raises an important issue: the explanation of a causal capacity will be narrow or wide depending upon whether the relevant causal properties are restricted to narrow ones or include wide ones. Such restrictions will depend upon the explanatory context. If I only want to explain the mechanical capacity of neuron A to cause muscles to retract, then of course I will be restricted to intrinsic properties. However, if I am an evolutionary biologist who wants to know how an organism has evolved to retract into its shell in the presence of predators, then I will need to include wide as well as (narrow) mechanical causal properties in my explanation. This does not require that neuron A "knows" anything about its causal ancestry, just that it is part of a wider causal system. The "width" of explanation here depends upon the explanatory project of the science at issue. Physiologists may be interested only in mechanical properties of the organism; evolutionary biologists may be interested in the relationship of the organism to its environmental niche, the phylogenetic history of the species of which the organism is a member and the ontogenetic history of the organism itself. This ought to be a salutary methodological lesson to individualists who espouse the principle of autonomy, or methodological solipsism.

Importantly, cognitive integrationists think that there are wide causal capacities, because some cognitive vehicles and processes are external. In the individualist's terms, some cognitive capacities will be wide, because they rely upon wide causal properties.[10] So we need to distinguish between narrow causal capacities that supervene only on intrinsic causal properties and wide causal capacities that supervene on both intrinsic and wide causal properties. This distinction is important for our consideration of Fodor's way of taxonomising by causal capacities.

Fodor argues that we need a way of determining what kind of causal properties are relevant to determining the causal capacities that a thing has.

> To classify by causal [capacities] is to count no property as taxonomically relevant unless it affects causal [capacities]. But x's having property P affects x's causal [capacities] just in case x wouldn't have caused the same events had it not been P. (1987, p. 38)

It is important to note that this definition of *affecting causal capacities* is the same for both intrinsic and wide properties. Hence, Fodor ought to adopt only the weak form of the premise – the causal capacities an entity has supervene upon the causal properties it has – but the weak premise is no support for the conclusion that cognitive capacites supervene on intrinsic properties of individuals.

Given this definition of the dependence of causal capacities on causal properties, there is a clear sense in which neuron A would not have caused the muscle contraction if it had not been selected to do so in the presence of predators. The wide causal capacity is dependent upon both intrinsic and wide properties.

It follows that wide and intrinsic properties will be irrelevant to taxonomy by causal capacities, when they do not affect the causal capacities that a thing has. It turns out that Fodor is quite willing to accept that taxonomy is often in terms of wide properties.

> it's patent that taxonomic categories in science are *often* relational. Just as you'd expect, relational properties can count taxonomically whenever they affect causal [capacities]. Thus "being a planet" is a relational property par excellence, but it's one that individualism permits to operate in astronomical taxonomy. For whether you are a planet affects your trajectory, and your trajectory determines what you can bump into; so whether you're a planet affects your causal [capacities], which is all that individualism asks for. (1987, p. 43)

This all seems ecumenical, both intrinsic and wide properties affect causal capacities; therefore, taxonomy will be by both wide and intrinsic properties. As we have seen, Fodor does concede that wide properties can *affect* the causal capacities a thing can have. This concession shows that there is no general motivation for the specific claim that cognitive causal capacities are individuated by intrinsic properties. It shows that the first stage of the argument is really no support for the second. Consequently we shall have to look elsewhere to support the claim that cognitive capacities supervene on intrinsic properties.

1.5.2 Causal capacities supervene on intrinsic causal properties

Given the arguments and concessions of the previous section, it looks clear that Fodor ought to accept the distinction between narrow causal capacities and wide causal capacities. This is because either the causal capacities a thing has are due to its intrinsic properties, or they are due to its wide properties, or they are due to a combination of the two. The final option is all that is required for a wide capacity.

However, Fodor also holds that the causal capacities that a thing has are due only to its intrinsic properties, call this a narrow causal capacity. The general notion that causal capacities can only be narrow is motivated by the general assumption that causal capacities are not constituted by wide properties (Stalnaker 1989).

The crucial caveat here is that wide properties must still affect intrinsic properties if they are to affect causal capacities; this is because, as Stalnaker (1989) puts it, environmental facts do not *constitute* causal capacities. The same metaphysical assumption is behind Fodor's claim that causal capacities must supervene upon intrinsic causal properties; hence he would reject the notion of wide causal capacities.

But he ought to accept the notion, so let us motivate it further by returning to the example of neuron A. Neuron A has the narrow capacity to cause muscle contraction, because it has the causal property of spiking at a particular threshold. However, neuron A also has the wide capacity of causing muscle contractions in the presence of predators. This is because, in the first instance, it has the intrinsic causal property of spiking at a particular threshold. Secondly, neuron A became activated in the ancestors of the organism which had it in the presence of predators and would not have become activated if the predator had not been present.[11] The wide capacity depends on both the intrinsic property of neuron A and the historical and wide properties that cause A to fire in the presence of predators.

Fodor ought to adopt the wide sense of causal capacities, because the organism would not be able to cause itself to retract into its shell in the presence of predators if it did not have both intrinsic and wide causal properties. The individuation of the wide causal capacity depends upon both intrinsic and wide properties. This means that some wide properties are properly causal properties in determining the causal capacities of a thing. According to Wilson, there certainly are biological cases where wide properties function as explanantia (as causes):

> For example, being a Mother, being unemployed, being a member of a particular species, being a planet, being located in a magnetic

field, and occupying a relatively specific ecological niche are all relational properties that different properties can have in particular instantiating circumstances, each of which, when coinstantiated with the appropriate properties, enables an entity to bring about particular effects. With respect to causal efficacy, some relational properties are *just like* paradigmatic intrinsic properties. . . . (Wilson 1995, p. 124)

Explanations that make reference only to narrow causal capacities allow us to refer only to the intrinsic causal properties of neuron A. This would be the construal that accords with the principle of autonomy.

The wide construal is dependent upon neuron A coming to have the biological function that it does. This would be a matter of selective pressures over generations, or a function acquired by learning or re-inforcement. In this case the explanation is by the wide causal capacity that the organism has which is dependent upon its historical relations to its environment (its wide properties). Therefore, the biological function of the organism to contract muscles in the presence of predators is dependent upon relations to the environment and it would not have the causal capacity of contracting muscles in the presence of predators if it did not have this wide property. All Fodor asks for a causal capacity to be dependent upon a causal property is that without that property the causal capacity would not be able to bring about its effect. So by Fodor's own definition, wide causal capacities are on the cards.

It follows that internalists, such as Fodor, ought to concede that there are both narrow and wide causal capacities. They should make this concession because the kind of explanation that a science requires will determine whether wide or narrow causal capacities are used as part of that explanation. However, if Fodor, or any other individualist, was to endorse the use of wide causal capacities, he would have to accept that they are constituted by both wide causal properties and intrinsic causal properties. Therefore, the cherished metaphysical assumption that only intrinsic properties can be truly causal cannot be used to motivate psychological individualism.

This accords with Wilson's notion of wide realisation. A wide realisation is one where a system extends beyond the boundary of the individual which has it (Wilson 2004, p. 112). The point can be made in terms of dispositions; Wilson points out that many dispositions in the physical sciences are relational (wide), whether or not a liquid is an acid is one such example. Being a particular chemical substance involves a disposition to have certain effects on other substances and the having of these dispositions is determined by the nature of those other substances (Wilson 2004).

> The very presence of the disposition, not just its manifestation, involves the physical configuration of the world beyond the bearer of the disposition. . . . This point is reflected in standard definitions of an acid – for example, as a proton donor, or as an electron-pair acceptor. For whether a substance with a given physical structure has the disposition to donate protons or to accept electron pairs depend upon facts about the broader chemical system in which that substance exists. If just these facts were different, a liquid that is actually an acid could lose this disposition, and could do so even were its chemical composition to remain unchanged. (Wilson 2004, pp. 125–6)

Fodor has to concede that there are wide causal capacities to be found even in the physical sciences, because some wide properties act as causal properties. However, he does not think that there can be wide psychological causal capacities. This is because, in the psychological case wide properties affect causal capacities only by affecting the intrinsic properties of an individual, he and Stich are as one on this. So I turn now to dealing with the third premise.

Premise 3: *In the psychological case the relevant causal properties supervene upon local neural structure.*

- *Methodological point*: Categorization in science is characteristically taxonomy by causal capacities. Identity of causal capacities is identity of causal consequences across nomologically possible contexts.
- *Metaphysical point*: Causal capacities supervene on local microstructure. In the psychological case, they supervene on local neural structure. (Fodor 1987, p. 44)

So far we have been dealing with the methodological point, but the metaphysical point is crucial. The causal capacities a thing has (what effects it can cause) supervene on local microstructure (in the case of psychology on neural structures). Fodor does not allow that causal capacities supervene upon wide properties and this coheres with the principle of autonomy. But why does Fodor think this?

> We abandon this principle at our peril; mind/brain supervenience (/identity) is our only plausible account of how mental states could have the causal powers that they do have. (Fodor 1987, p. 44)

The intuition at work here is obvious; only intrinsic properties are really causally efficacious, but this intuition is mistaken, as we have already seen. Consequently, the narrow version of the second premise of Fodor's argument is false, because causal capacities in general do not supervene exclusively on intrinsic properties. So, it looks increasingly likely that premise 3 will be false as well.

Returning to our example, the narrow causal capacity of neuron A to contract muscles in the presence of predators is dependent upon local neural structure. Neuron A is connected to muscles and must transmit electrochemical messages along these connections, before any contraction is possible. The wide causal capacity of the organism to retract into its shell in the presence of predators depends upon relational and historical properties of the organism, as well as intrinsic ones. The wide causal capacity of the organism supervenes upon both its intrinsic properties and its wide properties. The question is, are there any cognitive capacities that are wide in this sense?

Fodor thinks this is unlikely because there must be a mechanism to bring about any causal effects and the mechanism must be physical. In the psychological case, although relational properties will affect causal capacities and individuation will often be wide, the psychological mechanism specified must supervene on a physical/neural mechanism. Fodor stipulates that you cannot affect causal capacities of mental states, except via the physiology of the organism:

> you *can't* affect the causal powers of a person's mental states without affecting his physiology. . . . God made the world such that the mechanisms by which environmental variables affect organic behaviours run via their effects on the organism's nervous system. (Fodor 1987, p. 40)

Wide cognitive capacities might be like biological capacities that have been selected for, as in our simple example of neuron A; but they might be like the causal capacities of a planet. A planet has its causal capacities because of the present relations it has to other objects and forces in its environment. The planet's velocity is dependent on both its intrinsic properties and its wide properties. There is a mediating law or mechanism to allow the continual causal influence of the environmental factors. It follows that the relations a cognitive system stands in at any particular time may affect the causal capacities that it has.

For example, sensorimotor contingency and ecological accounts of perception depend upon wide properties. They depend upon continuous causal interaction between the ambient array of light, the movement of the body and the brain. What we perceive depends upon the continuous causal influence of environmental factors.

In Chapters 4, 5, 6 and 7, I provide a comprehensive range of examples of wide cognitive capacities. Therefore, Fodor's metaphysical claim that cognitive causal capacities supervene only on intrinsic properties is false.

Fodor holds that as long as a causal property affects causal capacities, then it is taxonomically relevant and this allows for individuation by wide properties. However, he assumes that the relevant psychological causal capacities supervene on the brain and that if wide properties are to affect causal capacities they must do so by affecting intrinsic properties of brains. This is because, only intrinsic properties of neural mechanisms are truly causally efficacious. The assumption of local supervenience of causal capacities on intrinsic properties is not global, because wide properties are often causally efficacious. Therefore, there are wide causal capacities.

It is then an open question whether or not there are wide cognitive capacities, but there is nothing in the argument from causal capacities which precludes them, except for an adherence to mind–brain supervenience. The evidence is stacking up against mind–brain supervenience; cognitive integrationists provide many examples of wide cognitive capacities, for which I direct the reader to Chapters 4, 5, 6 and 7.

1.6   First stage of the computational argument: Methodological solipsism

As we saw in the first section of this chapter, a methodological constraint follows quite naturally from mind–brain supervenience:

that the states and processes that ought to be of concern to psychological explanation are those that supervene on the current, internal, physical state of the individual. Methodological solipsism gives us a way of making this methodological constraint hold in computational cognitive science. The computational version of methodological solipsism depends upon what Fodor (1980) calls the "formality condition": computational processes have access only to the formal properties of representations and not the semantic ones, where semantic properties are taken to be wide properties. Solipsism is supposed to be derived from the formality condition, because formal properties, inevitably, supervene upon intrinsic properties of an individual, hence mind–brain supervenience holds.

Yet we can easily see how the formality condition is quite consistent with cognitive integration on the assumption that the manipulations of external vehicles have access to the formal properties of those vehicles.[12] Given that the vehicles are *externally located* and that they are manipulated externally, solipsism cannot follow. Therefore, cognitive science does not individuate cognitive states and processes narrowly (without reference to the environment). Consequently, even in computational cognitive science individualism does not hold. I shall now look at how methodological solipsism is argued for.

Putnam claims that the internalist conception of mind is based on an assumption of "methodological solipsism" which is derived from Descartes.

> This assumption is the assumption that no psychological state, properly so called, presupposes the existence of any individual other than the subject to whom that state is ascribed. (Putnam 1975, p. 10)

Descartes initiated a theoretical divide between mind and world, where an internal subject is related to an external world via a perceptual interface. This, of course, ultimately leads to a methodology for studying mind based upon the divide. Descartes was also an early exponent of the representational theory of mind (henceforth RTM): the internal mind is related to the external world by representations, ideas, causally connected via perceptual interfaces to the external environment.

Contemporary exponents of RTM, in cognitive science, claim that the mind supervenes on the brain. The representations and processes over those representations can safely be characterised as physical or supervening on the brain. This is a way of thinking about the mind that makes it "self-contained," from its environment. This is to say that the environment makes no essential difference *to the state of mind we are in* (Fodor 1980). It relies upon the thesis of the local supervenience of computational states on brain states, and the claim that the processing of representations has no immediate access to the external environment.

The methodological solipsist takes this Cartesian claim seriously. He distinguishes between a *rational* psychology and a *natural* psychology (Fodor 1980). The rational psychologist takes seriously the Cartesian injunction that the way the world is makes no essential difference *to the state of mind we are in.* (Fodor 1980) Naturalists, by contrast, focus on the fact that the organism is embedded in an environment and what the relevant organism–environment interactions are (Fodor 1980, p. 487). According to the methodological solipsist, we should only do rational psychology, because natural psychology is too difficult. This is so because natural psychology needs to explain organism–environment relations.

The natural psychologist has to provide law-like generalisations covering each of these relations by specifying the relation between an organism and an object in its environment, such that the organism is thinking about that object. As such the theory would need to

define its generalizations over mental states on the one hand and environmental entities on the other, it will need, in particular, some canonical way of referring to the latter. (Fodor 1980, p. 496)

Natural psychology would depend upon other sciences for the characterisation of the relation and the canonical description of the objects the organism is related to. This marks out the difficulty in doing natural psychology. Take the following example used by Fodor (1980, p. 496):

1. Salt is the object of what "Granny desires to put on her herring."
2. We rely on chemistry to give us a canonical description of salt as NaCl.

3. This requires that for all the other objects of thought there is a canonical description of the object forthcoming from one of the sciences.
4. This isn't true.
5. Therefore, natural psychology is too difficult.

Fodor's complaint is that natural psychology makes psychological methodology dependent upon other sciences. He takes this to be pernicious, because

> (a) that we don't know relevant nomologically necessary properties of most of the things we can refer to (think about) and (b) that it isn't the linguist's (psychologist's) job to find them out. (Fodor 1980, p. 496)

Therefore, we should restrict ourselves to a rational psychology. This conclusion applies not just to causal theories of content, but to any psychological theory that makes use of organism–environment relations in general, such as Gibson's ecological theory of perception. Of course, Fodor has changed his mind on this, he now endorses a natural psychology of content where the meaning of mental representations is determined by causal relations to environmental objects. Hence, natural psychology is on the cards even for Fodor.

We could restrict rational psychology to computational psychology where methodological solipsism depends upon the formality condition. Computational processes (and mental processes if they are computational) are both *symbolic* and *formal*:

> They are symbolic because they are defined over representations, and they are formal because they apply to representations, in virtue of (roughly) the *syntax* of the representations. (Fodor 1980, p. 486)

Syntactic operations are defined over a symbol's intrinsic physical properties, such as its shape. These operations are not sensitive to any of the semantic properties a symbol may have, that depend upon their relations to the environment. Fodor goes on to say that the

> Formality condition connects with the Cartesian claim that the character of mental processes is somehow independent of their

environmental causes and effects. If mental processes are formal, then they have access only to the formal properties of such representations of the environment as the senses provide. (1980, p. 488)

However, the formality condition does not establish methodological solipsism, because the computational vehicles and processes might be environmentally located. Only if we assume that computational processes and vehicles supervene upon internal neural structures can we make the formality condition count in favour of methodological solipsism. This follows if we take the doctrine of the local supervenience of the mind upon the brain to be true, but we have so far seen no good reason for accepting it (see the previous discussion on wide causal capacities). Let us try an example, from Kim Sterelny (1990, p. 35), to help clarify the claim.

My seeing a tree causes a visual representation, A, of that tree in my visual cortex. The visual representation A causes the representation, B, "that is an oak tree." Whilst the distal environment – the oak tree – caused A, B was caused *only* by A (even if A had been produced by a hologram). The causal ancestry of A is irrelevant to the tokening of B; this could only be the case if B comes about because of features of A which are narrow, or internal to the system. Computational processes do not have access to these relational properties of A.

As with neuron A (from the previous section), representations A and B are merely sequences in a long, albeit hugely simplified, causal chain. A different way of viewing the sequence would be to view the environment and "internal" representations as an integrated system, where causal interactions go both ways. The question though is why we should not do this?

As we have seen, the formality condition is consistent with the representations in question being located in the environment, because it is a condition only on the properties that computational processes have access to. The formality condition says nothing about mental representations and mental processes having to supervene upon the brain, this is assumed by the internalist.

As we shall see, in the next section, this is the main problem with the computational argument for internalism. The internalist asserts that the external physical and social environment of an individual have no constitutive relevance to that individual's mind. In methodological mode, psychological states are taxonomised in such a way that the nature of the external world of the individual is irrelevant. However, if vehicles of cognition supervene on the environment, then we must include the environment as well as the discrete individual in our cognitive explanations. Narrow individuation would fail in these cases, because psychological states would have to be individuated in such a way that the world is relevant to the state of mind we are in. Therefore, methodological solipsism restricts the explanatory framework of computational cognitive science in a pernicious way.

The computational argument, just like the argument from causal capacities, relies upon the truth of mind–brain supervenience and its truth is assumed.

1.7 The second stage of the computational argument: Integrated computational systems

Robert Wilson (1995, p. 64) provides a simple version of the computational argument for individualism:

(A) The sciences of cognition taxonomically individuate mental processes only qua computational processes.
(B) The computational states and processes that an individual instantiates supervene on the intrinsic states of that individual. Therefore,
(C) The sciences of cognition individuate states and processes that supervene on the intrinsic physical states of the individual who instantiates those states and processes.

This argument is unsound, if premise B is false. Cognitive integrationists think that it is false and that the conclusion does not follow. Premise A is quite possibly false as well if the notion of computation is too restrictive, see above for a discussion of pluralism about processing and vehicles in cognitive science. The computational arguments I will look at are based on a classical – that is not a connectionist – conception of computational processes and vehicles.

What we now need to do is find out why, if the cognitive system is a computational system, it is individualistic? Let us begin by asking what the computational theory of mind is committed to, before looking at Segal (1991) and Egan's (1992) versions of the argument.

A classical computationalist account of mental processes entails that there is a causal sequence of thoughts – A–B–C–D. Each thought is an explicit symbol token and each antecedent token is causally responsible for each consequent token.

A. Fred believes it is too hot in here.
B. Fred notices that the fire is on full.
C. Fred hypothesises that turning down the fire would reduce the heat in the room.
and
D. Fred desires to turn down the fire.
Causes:
E. Fred turns the fire down

Each thought is causally responsible for the next and this is only possible if

1. Each thought is explicitly tokened.
2. The causal relations between thoughts mirrors the semantic relations between thoughts.

If B was "Fred noticed that the sun was shining in through the window," then thoughts C and D would be different thoughts, in virtue of the content of B. Thinking involves a causal sequence of explicit thoughts, where the sequence is determined by what the thoughts mean.

We have seen what a sequence of thoughts is, but how do these thoughts get their causal capacities? They do so by being computational states. We can generally understand this in the following way. A computing machine is a device which has the following features:

• It contains media in which symbolic representations can be stored. These symbols can be arranged into expressions in virtue of their syntactic structure. The symbols mean something, they are interpreted.
• A computer can differentiate between symbols, via distinctions in their syntactic "shape."
• The computer can cause the tokening of new symbols.

- The causal processes that govern what new symbols will be tokened are dependent upon the syntactic form of the symbols already stored in the machine.

Imagine a computer which has the numbers 2 and 3 stored at locations A and B. A new tokening of a representation of a sum of these two numbers will be caused to occur at location C. The symbol tokened at C depends upon the symbols at A and B, but the new tokening at C is strictly dependent upon the syntactic form of the symbols at A and B and not upon their interpretations.

The interesting thing is that the semantic properties of the symbols play no causal role in the process. However, the claim is that the semantic distinctions between the symbols are preserved by the syntactic distinctions between the symbols, and the syntactic type of the symbol determines its causal role in a process.

Semantic properties can have a causal role indirectly because any semantic differences between symbols are reflected in their syntactic distinctions: for any two symbols S and S*, if they differ with respect to their semantic properties then, according to the computational theory, they must also differ with respect to their syntactic properties.

We can see how in a sequence of thoughts, consequent thoughts are dependent upon antecedent thoughts, because, as with the above example, the syntactic properties of the antecedent representations determine which consequent representations get tokened; and the semantic relations between antecedent and consequent representations are mirrored by the syntactical relations between the antecedent and the consequent representations.

Wilson sites Egan as an individualist who thinks that it follows from this characterisation of the computational theory of mind that it is individualistic in the way that it conceives of mental states and mental processes.

"Symbols are just functionally characterised objects whose individuation conditions are specified by a *realization function* f_R which maps equivalence classes of physical features of a system to what we might call 'symbolic' features. Formal operations are just those physical operations that are differentially sensitive to the aspects of symbolic expressions that under the realization function f_R are specified as symbolic features. The mapping f_R allows a causal sequence of physical state transitions to be interpreted as a *computation.*

Given this method of individuating computational states, two systems performing the same operations over the same symbol structures are computationally indistinguishable." From this she concludes that "if two systems are molecular duplicates then they are computational duplicates. Computational descriptions are individualistic – they type-individuate states without reference to the subject's environment or social context." (Egan 1992, p. 446)

Wilson notes (1995, p. 68) that Egan's conclusion only follows if we equate the computational system with an individual subject. This begs the question against cognitive integration, or Wilson's "wide computationalism".[13] The claim that mental states and mental processes must supervene on intrinsic properties of subjects does not follow from the formality condition (as we saw in the previous section). This is because the formality condition states only that, *Computational processes have access only to the formal properties of representations, such as their size and shape.* It does not state that representations and processes *must* supervene upon intrinsic properties of subjects, they could, in principle, be spread out over subject and embedding environment. So, that line of argument is now closed to the computational individualist.

Segal (1991) argues for an individualist reading of computational systems, by invoking the notion of an integrated computational system:

1. The representational states that a computational system is in are determined by the intrinsic properties of the system.
2. Computational systems are integrated.
3. The computational system is integrated in virtue of the supervenience base of properties, which the representational states and computational states of the system supervene upon.
4. The intrinsic properties of the supervenience base are the determinants of the representational states that the system is currently in as well as the state changes which the system is capable of.

As we have just noted, the first claim cannot be made via the formality condition. The individualist may just wish to *stipulate* that formal properties are intrinsic properties, because they supervene on intrinsic properties of individual brains. As such, this would preclude the extension of the computational system beyond the discrete individual. However, this is an entirely empirical claim, and if there are vehicles in the environment that are processed in terms of their formal properties, then these properties are not intrinsic to the individual.

Let us turn to the second point about integration. Internalists think that a computational system is physically integrated when all its components have a causal influence over one another. Cognitive integrationists accept that components must have a causal influence over one another, but reject that they *must* be located exclusively in the body.

The internalist is worried that if a cognitive system had some of its mental representations spread out beyond the boundary of the discrete individual, how would the cognitive processes which supervene on neural mechanisms get access to them? Computational processes would have remote access to these symbol structures, but this commits us to action at a distance, which is absurd. The simple response is that not all cognitive processes supervene on the brain, some processes are constituted by bodily manipulations of external representations and no action at a distance is implied by that.

The computational argument for internalism fails again. It leaves open the possibility that the cognitive integrationist could provide examples of external and internal cognitive processes having a causal influence over one another. This would be to show that the "cognitive system" is integrated even if some vehicles of cognition and the processing of those vehicles occurs outside the head. If the integrationist is right, as I hope to show, then the supervenience base of properties will include wide properties as well as intrinsic properties. Segal is willing to wager an empirical bet with the integrationist:

> Individualism is the thesis that the representational states of a system are determined by intrinsic properties of that system. It seems likely that whole subjects (or whole brains) make up large, integrated, computational systems. Whole subjects plus embedding environments do not make up integrated, computational systems. That is one reason why individualists draw the line where

they do: the whole subject is the largest acceptable candidate for the supervenience base because it is the largest integrated system available. (Segal 1991, p. 492)

This, like the other reasons given in this chapter, turns out not to be a good enough reason to be an individualist/internalist. In the second part of this book we will see numerous examples of the integration of internal and external vehicles and processes in the completion of cognitive tasks.

What the arguments for individualism show is that internalism about mental states and mental processes is motivated by the assumption of the local supervenience of the mind upon the brain. Cognitive scientists do not always respect local supervenience in their taxanomic and methodological practices. Like the metaphysical assumption that only intrinsic properties are causal, it is a bad assumption. There is nothing that precludes cognitive scientists breaking with the autonomy principle in practice – and they do so on a regular basis.

1.8 Conclusion

We have seen that cognitive internalism, as it is expressed in psychological individualism, relies upon the assumption of the local supervenience of the mind upon the brain: all cognitive properties, states and processes *must* supervene upon intrinsic properties of the brain. We have seen that there are two arguments for this kind of internalism: the argument from causal capacities and the computational argument for individualism in psychological explanation. Fodor hoped to show that causal capacities supervene *only* upon intrinsic properties of individuals, in this sense causal capacities are narrow. However, his argument allows for wide causal capacities and leaves open the possibility that there are wide cognitive capacities.

The computational argument assumes that local supervenience is a necessary condition for the computational theory of mind. Computational processes have access only to syntactical properties of representations, mental representations supervene upon the brain, and therefore computational processes must supervene upon the brain. This makes sense if we are worried about cognitive processes extending out beyond the boundary of the skin. This worry only holds if the internal and the external components of a cognitive system are not integrated, because its components must have a causal influence over one another. The computational argument also relies upon an empirical bet. As Segal reminds us, there just are no psychological theories that treat whole subjects plus embedding environments as integrated cognitive systems. This bet has been taken up and I know where my money lies.

Both arguments are refuted when we find evidence of cognitive causal capacities supervening upon wide properties and psychological theories which treat whole subjects and embedding environments as integrated cognitive systems. More and more of this kind of evidence is emerging from the cognitive sciences. This casts doubt on the reliance on mind–brain supervenience. We ought to have good reasons for accepting the local supervenience of the mind upon the brain, it should not merely be assumed as a dogma. In the next chapter, I will look at some definitions of externalism and outline the dynamical approach to integration.

2
Externalism, Dynamics and the Extended Mind

2.1 Introduction

In this chapter, I outline the dynamical approach that informs the notion of reciprocal coupling/causation. Especially important, for cognitive integration, is the way that two reciprocally coupled systems are treated as components of a larger system. I then go on to discuss the important difference reciprocal coupling makes to cognitive integration and why this differentiates it from its cousin externalism.

I then turn to active externalism and the extended mind. Clark and Chalmers (1998), henceforth C&C, argue that we should extend our conception of mind to include the environment. The first formulation of this thesis is found in "The Extended Mind" (Clark and Chalmers 1998) but Clark has written a series of papers and books in which the original formulation is expanded (Clark 2001b, c, 2003, 2005, 2007). The original formulation of the extended mind hypothesis has it that some processes and vehicles in the environment are part of our cognitive processing because: (a.) organism and environment are coupled in an interactive, or symmetrical relation, which creates a system that is a cognitive system in its own right and (b.) there is a parity of function between inner processes and vehicles and processes and vehicles in the environment.

Another formulation of the extended mind takes into account the complementarity of the internal and external cognitive resources necessary for their integration. There is a complementarity between what the biological brain can do and what the environment provides, such that inner processes and vehicles and outer processes and vehicles work together to complete a cognitive task (Clark 2001a, Clark 2003, Sutton 2007).

The parity-based approach to the extended mind does not include two important factors that are central to cognitive integration: the transformatory impact integration has on our cognitive capacities, both in the here and now and during cognitive development. On this view the external cognitive environment transforms what the individual can do cognitively, both synchronically and diachronically (Vygotsky 1978, Wertsch 1985). The other factor is the normativity of the manipulation of external vehicles in our cognitive practices.

In this chapter, I aim to show that a parity-based version of the extended mind, that relies upon causal coupling as its sole motivation, is insufficient for our purposes and is open to a number of internalist objections (which I shall outline and respond to in the next chapter). Fortunately, integration is not susceptible to the same internalist objections (as I shall show in the next chapter).

2.2 Integration and externalism

The dynamical approach tells us that bodily internal and external processes have a continuous reciprocal effect on one another. This sounds like a version of externalism, but there are asymmetric versions of externalism, where the direction of influence goes only one way. Since cognitive integration is based upon the dynamical notion of reciprocal coupling, it should not be confused with asymmetric versions of externalism.

A general definition of the externalist strategy is, *properties of a system or properties of components of a system are explained by features external to that system.* As such, externalists try to explain internal features of some defined system in terms of relations to features which are external to it. In the philosophy of biology, the philosophy of mind and philosophical theories of meaning, this general externalist explanatory strategy takes slightly different forms.

In the philosophy of biology the externalist strategy of explanation can be defined, following Godfrey-Smith (1996), as, *properties internal to an organic system are explained in terms of properties of the environment of the organic system.* For example, if a biological trait of an organism is an adaptation then it is explained in terms of the selective pressures of the environment upon that organism – which gave rise to the adaptation. The biological trait is an adaptation to the environment.

In the philosophy of mind, externalism can be defined as, *the content of mental states is determined by features of the external world and the relations between mental states and features of the external world.* Content externalism in the philosophy of mind is also a thesis concerning the individuation of mental states, following Colin McGinn (1989): *externalism holds that mental distinctions (distinctions of content) are grounded in worldly distinctions, that the former depends upon the latter, that mental individuation is to be explained by reference to worldly conditions.*

It thus regards the direction of individuation as running from the world to the mind. Accordingly, this individuation-dependence is deemed asymmetrical: *the world is individuatively basic with respect to the mind. It is in virtue of environmental differences that mental differences are established.*

The basic externalist explanatory strategy holds to, as does internalism, the fundamental distinction between properties internal to the system of interest and properties which are external to it. The difference is in the direction of explanation, for the internalist it is from the inside to the outside and for the externalist it is from the outside in. Hence Godfrey-Smith says,

> I view an externalist in some field as a person who thinks external factors are more important or more informative than internal. But everyone agrees that, in almost all real systems, there will be some role played by both internal and external. Both internal and external factors are individually necessary and neither is individually sufficient. The outcome is a consequence of the interaction of both factors. (Godfrey-Smith 1996, pp. 48–9)

The delicate interplay between internal and external factors is the unit of interest to the integrationist. Sometimes internal factors will be more important and sometimes external factors will be more important, but it is in the ways that body and world combine that integration gets cashed out. Therefore, "internal" and "external" do not have the same methodological and metaphysical loading that they do for internalists and externalists. It makes no difference that internal and external vehicles and processes may differ in important respects, each contributing something different to the completion of cognitive tasks. These different roles make the combination of internal and external processes so important – they can do things together that they cannot achieve alone.

The strong form of asymmetric externalism as defined by Godfrey-Smith is

> A program of explanation that explains internal properties in terms of external, and also explicitly or implicitly denies that these external properties are to be explained in terms of properties of the organic system. So what is denied is any significant level of feedback from the organic system on its environment. The organic system has its nature or trajectory determined by the environment, but the environment goes its own way. It is dynamically self-contained, rather than coupled to the organic system. (Godfrey-Smith 1996, p. 327)

Cognitive integrationists, by contrast, do not think either that the organism is dynamically self-contained from the environment or that the environment is dynamically self-contained from the organism. Organism and local environment are coupled and cannot be studied apart from one another. In Chapter 5, we shall see how this symmetrical understanding of organism–environment systems is important in biology.

An example of the symmetrical approach is the enactivist approach to perception. A programmatic statement of this approach can be found in the following:

> We propose as a name enactive to emphasize the growing conviction that cognition is not the representation of a pregiven world by a pregiven mind but is rather the enactment of a world and a mind on the basis of a history of the variety of actions that a being in the world performs. (Varela, Thompson and Rosch 1991, p. 9)

Enactivism is based on the notion of cognition as emerging out of embodied action. Cognition emerges from processes of perception and action that give rise to recurrent sensorimotor patterns. Thus the enactive approach consists of two points:

(1) perception consists in perceptually guided action and (2) cognitive structures emerge from the recurrent sensorimotor patterns that enable action to be perceptually guided. The overall concern . . . is not to determine how some perceiver independent world is to be recovered; it is, rather, to determine the common principles or lawful linkages between sensory and motor systems that explain how action can be perceptually guided in a perceiver-dependent world. (Varela, Thompson and Rosch 1991, p. 173)

As such, enactivists hold that for an agent to be cognitive, it must have a body; and that the embodied agent is embedded in an environment such that it must be able to interact with that environment. Perception is understood in terms of dynamical causal loops between the organism and its environment, rather than as an asymmetrical relation.

Cognitive integration is dependent upon a notion of reciprocal coupling, which is a symmetrical relation between "internal" components and "external" components. This is because it is influenced by the dynamical conception of reciprocal coupling which takes parts of a system to be integrated because they are symmetrically dependent upon one another (as I will explain in the next section). Thus, cognitive integration can be differentiated from externalism when the relation between "internal" and "external" components is deemed to be asymmetric.

2.3 Cognitive dynamics

The notion of reciprocal causal coupling (Clark 1997) is based upon concepts from dynamical systems approaches to understanding organism–environment relations. Analysing cognitive systems as dynamical systems is an important methodological and conceptual resource for cognitive integration. This is because brains, bodies and aspects of the environment can all be treated as dynamical systems, and given interactions between them, they can also be treated as parts of a single overall system – the organism–environment system. Consequently, we have a methodology, which treats what were before only separate systems as parts of the same system. As I shall show in Chapter 5, there are also good biological and evolutionary reasons for taking this approach.

What concepts and tools does the dynamical approach use? The dynamical approach is understood in terms of what it is to be a dynamical system and to understand this we must turn to dynamical systems theory.

When is a system a dynamical system? First, we must begin with the notion of a system. A system is composed of parts, and if we assume that those parts interact with one another, then a change in one part will depend upon the state of the other parts. Thus, for a set of parts to be a dynamical system they must be *interactive*; that is, a change in a part of the system must depend upon, and only upon, other parts of the system. This dependence is symmetrical. It follows that if anything external interacts with a part of the system in this way, it must really be part of the system. Some obvious examples, given this understanding of system, are the solar system and the nervous system. Take this to be a working definition of an integrated system.

Added to this, we must consider how the states of the system change over time. The behaviour of the system is characterised as the change over time in its overall state (Port and van Gelder 1995, p. 5). To be able to understand how a dynamical system behaves over time we must have

1. A finite number of state variables, which define the state of the system at a particular time.
2. A set of state space evolution equations, which describe the changes of those variables over time.

A geometric model of all the possible states of the system can be given for (1), which we have already called its state space and each possible state of the system is given by a point in the state space. Given a point in the state space as a starting point, change in the state of the system is plotted as a trajectory through the state space – such trajectories are known as phase portraits. The continuous behaviour of the system is defined by the current state of the system – its position in state space – and the set of evolution equations which determine and describe the change in state variables over time. Understood in this way, cognitive processes and their context unfold continuously and simultaneously in real time.

The task of a dynamical analysis of a system is to define the equations of evolution that determine how the system will behave given its present state. In other words, we specify the ongoing behaviour of a dynamical system by its current state, and the evolution equations that govern how the system changes through time (Wheeler 1996, p. 223).

Following Randall Beer (Beer 1995), we can think of a coupled dynamical system in the following way:

An agent and its environment are modelled as two continuous-time dynamical systems – an agent A and its environment E. Although we are distinguishing between A and E, sometimes we will consider A's body to be a part of E. However, because A and E are constantly interacting they are described as non-autonomous dynamical systems. Beer simply represents this coupling in terms of a sensory function S from environmental variables to agent parameters and a motor function M from agent variables to environmental parameters. The two coupled systems affect one another through a constant process of feedback. An agent acts and affects its environment through M; this in turn affects the agent from the environment through S, which in turn affects the environment through M and so on.

The next move is an important one, which is to view these coupled systems as part of a wider system U. A and E are components of an autonomous system U. The state space of U contains all the variables of A and E, including S and M. Because of the higher dimensionality of its state space, a dynamical system formed by coupling two other systems can generate a richer range of dynamical behaviour than could either subsystem in isolation.

Therefore, U constitutes a wider system than A or E taken alone. U is the system constituted of A and E coupled via the continuous interactions of S and M. Why should we consider A and E as parts of a wider system U? Why not simply identify A and E as autonomous systems that occasionally influence one another? Because only by considering A and E as parts of a wider system can we understand the global properties and behaviours that arise from their interaction.

These properties and behaviours are beyond the ability of either subsystem taken on its own. This point is important for understanding cognitive integration, because integrationists argue that the cognitive unit is an unfolding dynamical system composed of internal processes over vehicles that interact with external processes over vehicles. The global behaviour of the system is a product of internal and external processes interacting and working in concert

(Wheeler 2005, p. 94). Compare this with the narrow metaphysical conception of causal capacities from the last chapter. Basing cognitive integration in the empirical conception of interacting dynamical systems is preferable to the a priori metaphysical assumptions that ground internalism. This is preferable if cognitive integration is to be consistent with empirical work and have consequences for future empirical work.

A real example of an artificial life form, which is coupled to its environment in the requisite sense, is Herbert. Herbert navigates his environment with the sole purpose of collecting things. He has to avoid bumping into objects, as well as to find, and identify the things he has been instructed to collect. He does not have a stored internal map or model of his environment for navigation. Herbert can maintain an internal state for no longer than 3 seconds, therefore Herbert has the memory of a goldfish. Herbert was implemented in a subsumption architecture (Brooks 1991), which consisted of independent layers composed of finite-state machines which operated asynchronously. Interestingly, in contrast to earlier robots such as Allen, the components (finite state machines) of each layer had no internal connections and did not communicate directly with each other.

Rather, Brooks claims that the world itself was the only effective medium of communication (Brooks 1991, p. 413). Herbert used 30 infrared proximity sensors to navigate the office environment, a magnetic compass for a sense of direction, a laser scanner to find cans and an arm with many extra sensors and behaviours for can collection. Each behaviour-generating module was connected to input sensors and an arbitration network which controlled the actuators, for movement and arm movement.

The claim that the components did not communicate with one another might lead us to expect that Herbert's behaviours could not be very complex or interesting. However, Herbert was able to negotiate its environment and adapt to changes in the environment flexibly. For example, the laser can detector oriented the robot such that its arm would be lined up with the can. The arm controller was not informed that there was a can in front of it, as we might expect, instead arm motion was initiated only when body motion had stopped. There were no internal expectations as to what was supposed to happen, there was no complicated interplay between behaviour-generating modules, there were no internal maps of the environment and there was no control centre issuing commands to peripheral motor modules (Clark 1997).

Brooks was interested in producing flexible real-time behaviour in a real environment, not simulated on a computer, emerging from the input-driven behaviour-producing components. However, the continuous causal interaction between sensors, environment and actuators produced the global properties of behaviour.

Brooks (1991) gives the following commitments to the dynamical approach to cognition:

The world is its own best model: Brooks admits that he has no particular interest in demonstrating how human beings work. Even if Brooks is exclusively interested in building autonomous robotic agents, some of his ideas about how to proceed in this endeavour are revealing of a philosophical position vis-à-vis an action-oriented approach to representation. This is primarily because they are a mode of an agent's engagement with the world, which is prior to that agent's construction of representations of the world (Wheeler 2005). We should be aware that Brooks takes the above slogan seriously, nothing else other than autonomous agents acting intelligently in this world, our world, will satisfy him.

We should also note that the extended mind has been greatly influenced by this slogan (Clark 1997, Wheeler 2005). It leads to rejecting the need for complex internal representations of the environment to produce flexible behaviours. Instead it directs us to explaining cognition in terms of the direct interaction between the organism and its local environment. This can also lead us to seek for complex representations in the environment, rather than in the head. Situatedness, embodiment and emergence are the other main concepts which define Brooks's approach.

Situatedness: Brooks's attack on traditional artificial intelligence (AI) is based upon its lack of real world inputs, compounded by the fact that the agents constructed by traditional AI are not even situated in the real world. Brooks claims that traditional AI agents are essentially problem solvers, and these problem solvers work in an abstract symbolic domain. They are fed symbolic inputs, which have been arbitrarily constructed by the engineers of the system. The symbols may have referents for the engineers, but there is nothing to ground those referents in the real world for the system itself.

We might elaborate on this by saying that there is nothing to which the symbols refer for the system, in the sense that there is no world of referents which the system has access to. The symbols chosen by the engineers have referents in their world, but the system has no access to that world, it has no genuine perceptual system, therefore there is no world in which the system's symbols are grounded. As such, we have a purely syntactical machine, an automated formal system, and this is inadequate in Brooks's view. As stated above, he is interested in autonomous agents which can navigate and act within this world; for him sequential acts of problem solving in a disembodied realm of interpreted symbols does not constitute autonomous agenthood. They are not participating in a world at all, as do agents in the usual sense.

Embodiment: Intelligent systems must be embodied to be able to be situated in their environment. The embodied system, an agent, must have an ongoing participation in and perception of the world, this is the only way the agent can in fact deal with the real world. Furthermore, Brooks claims that processing within the system can be given meaning only by direct perception of and participation in the world as an embodied agent. Simulated environments are not allowed.

Emergence: Intelligence emerges from the interactions of the behaviour-based components. There is no central processor or planning component. Each component, for obstacle avoidance or gaze control, is directly tied to producing the behaviours of avoiding obstacles and controlling gaze. Intelligent functions, such as planning and learning, emerge from the interactions of the behaviour-based modules. In contrast, Brooks says that traditional AI models have components for planning and learning, and behaviours such as avoiding obstacles and controlling gaze emerge out of the interactions of these components.

However, Brooks is eager to expand on this dualism between traditional and behaviour-based AI. Traditional systems are rarely connected to the world, and so the emergence of intelligent behaviour is, in most cases, more of an expectation than an established phenomenon (1991, p. 419). In contrast, behaviour-based models are embodied and situated in the world and we can talk of the emergence of intelligent behaviour in these agents as an established phenomenon. It is not feasible to identify the seat of intelligence within any system, since intelligence is produced by the interactions of many components. Intelligence can only be determined by the total behaviour of the system and how that behaviour appears in relation to the environment. (Brooks 1991, p. 419)

Therefore, the dynamical approach to cognition is important in giving cognitive integrationists the explanatory resources necessary to explain how we manipulate external cognitive vehicles. This is because it takes inspiration from the idea of two constantly interacting systems, whose global behaviour is continuously unfolding. Secondly, those systems are part of a wider system whose global behaviour arises out of the interaction of its component systems. It takes seriously the idea that cognitive agents are embodied and situated and that cognition often involves direct interaction with the bodily external environment, rather than the processing of bodily internal representations. However, cognitive integration parts company with more radical versions of the dynamical approach to cognition, which deny the need for any representations in cognition at all. Otherwise, cognitive practices would be irrelevant.

I turn now to active externalism and the extended mind, where the notion of reciprocal coupling is put to use.

2.4   Active externalism and causal coupling

In their paper "The Extended Mind," C&C hope to demonstrate that, as they say, "cognitive processes ain't (all) in the head!" (1998, p. 8) They claim that we must begin to extend the concept of cognition to include the active role of the environment in driving cognitive processes. The extension of cognition to include the role of the environment depends upon their thesis of active externalism: the environment plays an active, as opposed to a passive, role in cognition. It is the active character of this externalism which differentiates it from the meaning externalism of Putnam and Burge, because the relevant external features play an active role in the here and now (Clark and Chalmers 1998, p. 8). The move from the active role of external vehicles to extended cognitive processes depends upon the causal coupling of the individual to external vehicles.

C&C's answer is that active externalism uses a notion of mind and environment as a coupled system:

> In these cases, the human organism is linked with an external entity in a two-way interaction, creating a coupled system that can be seen as a cognitive system in its own right. (Clark and Chalmers 1998, p. 9)

This is a definition of what a coupled system is and is a move towards a more concrete account of how the causal interaction between an individual and an external entity constitutes a cognitive process.

For example, C&C take the re-arrangement of scrabble tiles on a tray, so as to better recognise whether the letters can be organised into a word, *to be part of thought* (Clark and Chalmers 1998, p. 10). This is because the scrabble tiles are external vehicles and their manipulation is part of an extended cognitive process. Therefore, active externalism is a constitutive thesis, it is not a matter of the asymmetric causal influence of the environment on internal processes.

C&C suggest that their examples of active externalism illustrate "the general tendency of human reasoners to lean heavily on environmental supports" (Clark and Chalmers 1998, p. 8). They point to the use of external media in cognition, so pen and paper are used in mathematical cognition and nautical slide rules are used in nautical cognition, in a more general sense the "paraphernalia" of books, diagrams, symbols, pictures are all important to various domains of cognition. Importantly, C&C go on to say that

> In all these cases the individual brain performs some operations, while others are delegated to manipulations of external media. Had our brains been different, this distribution of tasks would doubtless have varied. (Clark and Chalmers 1998, p. 8)

However, cognitive internalists can accept that there are external resources to aid cognition, as well as a class of actions which have the purpose of simplifying a problem – such as the re-organising of the scrabble tiles. This leaves them free to deny that there are any good grounds for identifying them as cognitive. External artefacts are often used as additions to short-term memory – the page serving as a storage device for long numbers, diaries for places and dates, shopping lists and so on. Of course, we use external media to write things down to remind ourselves what to do, or which things we need to acquire, but intuitively I do not count my shopping list as part of an extended cognition – this is supposed to cohere with common sense.

Similarly, a calculator is just a device we use for making calculations, it is not a part of my cognitive system and it is not a cognitive mechanism which underlies the process of mathematical reasoning. Hence, it cannot be part of a cognitive process and C&C are wrong to think that because I am causally related to an artefact, that it constitutes a cognitive process. Too many things would become cognitive if all we require is a causal relation to them. This is why cognitive integration requires the causal relation to be a bodily manipulation and for it to be governed by norms for manipulating an external vehicle in the completion of a cognitive task.

C&C could respond by arguing that cognitive processes are individuated by causal role, so if an external process plays the same causal role as an internal process, then they are functionally the same process. As such, if the external process is implicated in completing a cognitive task, then that external process is a cognitive process.[1]

So, if the cognitive task is to remember what I need to buy when I go shopping, then the role played by the shopping list is part of the extended cognitive process by which I complete the task. This is closer to the wider manipulation-based account which is at the heart of integration. This is to move away from the shadowy idea, deployed by internalists against the extended mind, that external vehicles and processes are cognitive simply because they are causally coupled to an individual.

However, the notion of coupling between active features of the external environment and the organism will not establish the extended mind on its own. We need more than just a causal account of the coupling relation if we are to have genuinely cognitive processes and vehicles, because we also need to take into account the normativity of cognition. Contrast reciprocal coupling, a description of a symmetrical causal relationship, with a "manipulation." A manipulation of an external vehicle goes beyond a simply causal relation because the manipulation needs to be described in terms of norms, and very often, content.

When I manipulate mathematical symbols on a page, I am already dealing in mathematical norms and interpretable symbols. Reciprocal coupling on its own will not explain what I am doing; therefore we need to put the coupling relation in a wider normative context.

Motivating integration by manipulation is easy. Imagine, for example, forming letters into a word without the benefit of re-organising the scrabble tiles, or writing them down with pen and paper and so on. In these cases it is the way that external artefacts are manipulated to complete the cognitive task that is important – being a cognitive agent involves being able to use external vehicles to complete cognitive tasks.

Cognitive processes are enabled by tools such as pens, and a description in terms of reciprocal coupling is part of the integrative explanation. Completing a mathematical task will involve writing down numbers on a piece of paper, but it will also involve following mathematical norms which specify how those numbers are to be written down and manipulated to complete the task. So any account of mathematical cognition will need to explain how we learn to use mathematical notations and how this is applied, along with tool use, in particular cases of mathematical problem solving.

Once we understand these processes in terms of our cognitive practices – problem solving, making inferences, planning and remembering things – there is no question of cognition being "internal," indeed we are no longer obsessed with the metaphysical questions of location and constitution. This is the answer to the internalist that comes from integrationist arguments concerning the importance of cognitive practices, rather than parity- and coupling-based extended mind style arguments.

Perhaps an example will help to illustrate the point. External media and re-structuring of the environment may actively drive cognition as C&C put it, but why must we concede that they are part of a cognitive process? The relevant parts of the world are in the loop, not dangling at the other end of a long causal chain. Yet there are many parts of the world which we may identify as being in the loop, but we are disinclined to count as extended cognitive processes. For example, the keyboard on which I type, the phone by which I speak to friends, the calculator on which I do calculations and so on.

C&C provide conditions for determining what a coupled system is

1. All components play an active causal role.
2. They jointly govern behaviour in the same sort of way that cognition does.

3. Removing the external component results in a drop in behavioural competence.
4. It is in this sense that the external features of a coupled system play an ineliminable role.

Now I shall take this definition and place it in an integrationist framework. The active features of the environment have an influence over us in the here-and-now. If we maintained the internal structure but varied the nature of the environment, then our behaviours and competences might alter radically. Causal coupling involves a kind of reciprocal influence, the inner and the outer features have a mutually constraining causal influence on one another which unfolds over time. For example, it is not simply that the written sentences in a diary prompt or cause, as input, various cognitive processes to unfold in my brain; it is rather that the external process of retrieving the information from the diary and the concurrent processes in my brain jointly govern my future behaviour.

This is the dynamical basis for cognitive integration. Although we can identify the relevant components, and factorise them into internal and external components, the nature of reciprocal coupling makes it difficult to study the components as separate systems because they are continuously influencing and responding to one another. They are co-ordinating with one another to produce behaviour. In so far as brain, body and world can be shown to be reciprocally coupled in this way, we can consider them to be a coupled system.

Take the example of writing a scholarly paper by word processing. Which of the components play an active causal role? Presumably, thanks to the CPU, the keyboard and monitor are able to exert an effect on what I write next and the words I type which come up on the screen are an extension of short-term memory. In a stronger sense, reading and re-reading what I have written gives me new ideas about what I should write next. Thus, the keyboard and monitor play an important causal role in the production of the paper. There is, however, a sense in which this is the wrong focus of interest.

Whilst it is true that tools such as keyboards and pens enable me to write, it is manipulating the written vehicles themselves that drives my cognitive processes. The sentences extend my working memory and are, of course, what can be re-written, erased, moved to another paragraph and so on. It is, moreover, precisely these kinds of manipulations that are not easily, if ever, achieved in the head.

Therefore, writing as an active and creative process is enabled by tools such as pen and paper or word processors. The written vehicles are then available for further manipulations such as restructuring, revising and re-drafting. Manipulating written vehicles is a kind of problem solving where a particular goal is aimed at: "how do I make this piece of writing clearer?", for example. I could, of course, compose a paper without external media. Nevertheless, not only would retaining the paper and updating it be made more difficult but, perhaps more crucially, it would take on different content and be written in a different style. The kind of manipulations of written sentences described above require external vehicles and tools for manipulating them, without them behavioural competence will drop.

However, it is not just a matter of ease that is at issue here; in an important sense, the manipulation of scripts transforms the skills needed in composing scholarly articles. The media function as enabling hardware, but the vehicles themselves enable processes that cannot be completed in the head alone. The physical act of typing[2] necessarily involves external physical manipulations. My ability to compose a paper is severely curtailed by the absence of those external manipulations. Hence, cognitive integrationists are inclined to think that those external manipulations play an important enabling role in the processing of the task.

Why could not we stick to a form of neural internalism here? There is, of course, an attenuated sense in which I can compose an article in my head. The likelihood of retaining much of the argument and structure would, however, become very limited. Making revisions and corrections would be almost impossible, for example trying out ideas and then deleting them. By contrast, becoming integrated with external tools and representations transforms my cognitive capacity to compose a philosophy paper. Importantly, there are things I can do with pen, paper or word processor that I cannot do in my head. Stable and enduring external written sentences allow for manipulations, transformations, re-orderings, comparisons and deletions of text that are not available to neural processes.

A further internalist worry becomes apparent here, why should the integrationist insist that the functioning of the tools and written sentences be cognitive? Why can not we just say that some of the representations and manipulations of those representations get manipulated in the environment and then function as input for further, genuine neural cognitive processes? Here we reach the nub of the issue, once the internalist accepts that the manipulation of representational vehicles is part of the process, it is very difficult for them to discount their cognitive function without invoking some form of neural chauvinism. Furthermore, the claim that manipulating written vehicles simply provides new input for neural processes does not do justice to the tightly coupled dynamical interactions between neural processes, bodily processes and manipulations of vehicles.

The active external components are cognitive because they actively drive the process of writing as described under conditions 1 and 2. The act of typing contributes to composition in a way that is manifestly different from my attempting to compose without the external tools described under conditions 3 and 4. The manipulations I can perform on external vehicles go beyond what I can achieve neurally. As such, there is a clear sense in which writing goes beyond simple external storage, it is thought in action.

Perhaps we are beginning to see how the causal coupling of a cognitive agent to external resources could constitute a case of cognitive integration, but it remains to be seen whether the conditions will cover more difficult cases as adequately.

In a telephone conversation, the telephone plays an active causal role, it mediates a conversation between an interlocutor and I. The telephone actively influences what I will hear and what my interlocutor will hear at the other end. If we remove the telephone, my behavioural competence will drop. It looks like the telephone is actively driving my cognition in C&C's sense, at least for as long as the conversation lasts. Should we want to accept this conclusion? I think it unlikely that we would want to include devices such as telephones, televisions and calculators as being part of our extended cognitive system, just because they have a causal influence over us. I think that the mistake in these cases is to think that the tools, or media, themselves should be counted as cognitive. The keyboard, the calculator, the telephone and the pen and paper are not cognitive, their having a mere causal influence on us is not sufficient for us to count them as cognitive.

However, if we focus on cognitive vehicles as external representations, and show how manipulations of the external vehicle is required to complete a cognitive task, such as the composition example above, then active externalism looks more plausible. This requires the wider context of cognitive integration, that there is a specific cognitive task that must be completed by manipulations of external vehicles.

Let us now turn our attention to the parity principle; here I think there are serious problems for the extended mind.

2.5 The parity principle

C&C begin to motivate the extended mind hypothesis further by the use of a parity principle:

> If, as we confront some task, a part of the world functions as a process which, *were it done in the head*, we would have no hesitation in recognizing as part of the cognitive process, then that part of the world *is* (so we claim) part of the cognitive process. (Clark and Chalmers 1998, 8)

This is supposed to be an intuition pump, a way of overcoming Cartesian prejudices (Clark 2005, p. 2). It is not, in itself, an argument for the extended mind. Rather, it asks us to consider why we would deny a process cognitive status just because it is external.

> But if an inner mechanism with this functionality would intuitively count as cognitive, then (skin-based prejudices aside) why not an external one? (Clark 2005, p. 7)

Care must be taken with the scope of the parity principle and its application as a supporting strand in extended mind style arguments. Problems arise because C&C's formulation of the parity principle does not rule out the misleading interpretation of the extended mind as "the externalising of internal processes." Nor does it rule out identifying external processes/vehicles as cognitive because of the relevant similarity of the external with the internal. For example, in comparing the use of a notebook with recall from biological memory, Clark says the following:

The right kind of coupling to make the resource into a part of the cognitive system, we argued, was one that poised the information contained in the notebook for sufficiently easy, reliable and automatic "use" (deployment would be a better word) *in much the same way as is typically (though not always) achieved by biological encoding.* (Clark 2007, forthcoming, my italics)

Most commentators and critics take this to be the point of the parity principle:

Clark and Chalmers' 1998 article leans heavily on the *parity argument*, which says that if a process counts as cognitive when it is performed in the head, it should also count as cognitive when it is performed in the world. (Dartnall 2005, pp. 135–6)

They [C&C] contend that the active causal processes that extend into the environment *are just like the ones found in intracranial cognition.* (Adams and Aizawa 2001, p. 56).

This interpretation is an error. External processes and vehicles do not get to have cognitive status conferred on them because they are relevantly *similar* to (supposedly) uncontroversial cases of cognitive processes and vehicles which are internal. Nor do they get to be relevantly similar because external processes and vehicles are causally coupled to internal processes/vehicles. Parity will not necessarily come from the direct similarity of the external with the internal. Internal process X may have properties a, b, c and external process Y may have properties d, e, and f. Internalists latch on to these differences and use them to deny parity and, therefore, that there are any external cognitive processes and vehicles.

This version of the parity principle is fatally flawed because it assumes the very position it is meant to displace. The "extended mind" and the parity principle encourage us to think of an internal cognitive system that is extended outwards into the world. Hence it implicitly endorses a picture of a discrete cognitive agent, some of whose cognitive processes get extended out into the world. The main question of the extended mind would then be, "How do bits of the world get to be like what's in the head?"

A major difference between extended mind style arguments and cognitive integration is that the latter does not depend upon the parity principle. It cannot be misinterpreted as claiming that cognition is extended from inside the head out into the world, or that external processes are cognitive because they are similar (weak version) or isomorphic (strong version) to internal processes. By contrast, I have been taking the following definition of a cognitive process which is agnostic as to location as standard throughout the book:

> *A process is cognitive when it aims at completing a cognitive task; and it is constituted by manipulating a vehicle.*

Again, cognitive integration differs from extended mind style arguments because it takes the manipulation thesis to be its starting point, not the parity principle. Clark clearly is committed to the manipulation thesis:

> In all these cases the individual brain performs some operations, while others are delegated to manipulations of external media. Had our brains been different, this distribution of tasks would doubtless have varied. (Clark and Chalmers 1998, p. 8)

Both Clark (1997, 2001a) and Rowlands (1999, 2003) explain the manipulation thesis by causal interaction between organism and environment, which they often refer to as causal coupling. While the parity principle is dispensable, the account of interactivity or causal coupling is crucial to understanding cognition as manipulating external cognitive vehicles.

However, as I have been arguing, the notion of manipulation includes normative factors not found in the stripped down relation of causal coupling. An embodied and normative account of manipulation, as a hybrid cognitive process, will be developed in Chapters 4, 5 and 6.

Let us clear up these issues here. Clark and Chalmers (1998) take external artefacts[3] to play the role of cognitive vehicles and they take the external manipulations of those vehicles to play the role of cognitive processes. C&C think that when Otto accesses his notebook to recall the address of the Museum of Modern Art (MOMA), this is *equivalent* to the recall of a memory to Inga, who uses only her biological memory capacities.

Integrating external vehicles in Otto's notebook with internal vehicles constitutes a part of the same cognitive system. In part because there is a reciprocal causal loop between them such that they have a mutual causal influence upon one another. In addition, the co-ordinated causal coupling allows the cognitive agent to complete the cognitive task. In this case the cognitive agent, Otto, manipulates the vehicles in his notebook to retrieve the desired information concerning the location of MOMA. Therefore, the cognitive integrationist claims that for any cognitive system, some cognitive vehicles and cognitive processes are externally located. Nevertheless, the overall cognitive system is integrated because "internal" and "external" vehicles have a causal influence over one another.

Now let us place the integrated cognitive system in a wider context. The cogniser finds herself in a situation where completing a cognitive task involves manipulating external vehicles. Here, we will need to give an account of the causal integration of manipulations of external vehicles with manipulations of internal vehicles.

However, we will also need an account of the cognitive norms by which we come to be able to manipulate external vehicles at all. There are norms governing manipulations of external representations, which aim at completing cognitive tasks. This is obvious given that external vehicles, such as written language and mathematical symbols,[4] are tokens of representational systems. Such systems have their own norms governing manipulations of token representational vehicles. Hence, they are cognitive norms, as opposed to moral or social norms. I shall call manipulations of an external representation to complete a cognitive task a *cognitive practice*. Otto's cognitive practice involves writing things in his notebook and then accessing them later. Otto's cognitive practice also falls under the definition of a cognitive process given above.

Therefore, manipulations of internal and external vehicles are causally integrated (pace Segal's internalist construal of integrated cognitive systems from the previous chapter), but we should place this within a wider cultural and normative context.

Cognitive integration benefits from the central insight of the extended mind hypothesis – some cognitive vehicles are bodily external and manipulations of these vehicles are part of the overall cognitive process, which includes manipulations of bodily internal vehicles. Cognitive integration goes further than the extended mind hypothesis, because it explains how external cognitive vehicles are manipulated in a wider context where we engage in cognitive practices to complete cognitive tasks. The final issue concerns parity versions of the extended mind as a commitment to the functional similarity of internal and external processes.

2.6 Functional similarity

The parity-based formulation of the extended mind is a functionalist thesis, take the Otto example. C&C want to say that in the case of Otto and Inga there is a sufficient *functional similarity* between Otto's use of his notebook and Inga's recall from biological memory that we are inclined to say that Otto has beliefs. Otto's retrieval of information about the location of MOMA causes him to go to 53rd street and the pattern of activation in a part of Inga's brain causes her to go to 53rd street. Otto's information retrieval and Inga's neural activations play the same kind of causal role in producing actions. As such, the physical implementation of the causal role is irrelevant to the functional level of description – Otto's use of his notebook and Inga's pattern of activation in her brain. Otto receives input from the environment, there is an exhibition on at the MOMA, he then retrieves the location of MOMA from his extended memory system, which causes him, as behavioural output, to go to 53rd street.

Only at the grossest level of functional description can this be said to be true. Otto and his notebook do not really function in the same kind of way that Inga does when she has immediate recall from biological memory. There are genuine and important differences in the way that memories are stored internally and externally and these differences matter to how the memories are processed. John Sutton has pointed out that biological memories stored in neural networks are open to effects such as blending and interference (see Sutton 2007 for discussion). The vehicles in Otto's notebook, by contrast, are static and do no work in their dispositional form (Sutton 2007).

This is of course no problem for cognitive integration, which does not work from the assumption that internal and external vehicles and processes need to be functionally equivalent. They may function in very different ways, as Sutton points out. However, this is the point, it is because the external vehicles provide a different kind of functionality and that they can co-ordinate with internal processes that they are integral parts of our cognitive systems. Again, putting this complementary integration in the wider context of cognitive tasks and practices highlights the cognitive roles that external vehicles can play; but this is not a matter of functional similarity.

2.7 Conclusion

What I hope to have shown in this chapter is that the central insights of extended mind style arguments can be defended and incorporated into a wider set of theses that constitute cognitive integration.

The integrationist takes the kind of coupled processes that C&C identify as evidence of there being an important relationship between an individual and her environment and then places these interactions in a wider context. People learn how to manipulate external representations with pens and paper and learn to read and write, make lists, plans, notes, diagrams and so on and they learn to do these things for particular purposes. Often the ability to manipulate external tools and representations allows us to solve problems in a way that we would not without them. This is certainly the moral of active externalism, however it is not explained solely by there being a causal influence of the artefacts over the individual. There are far too many things that have a causal influence on us that are not involved in our cognitions. We would be better off thinking of the extended mind as a set of abilities to use tools and representational systems, such as language, or logical and mathematical notations, or diagrams. These abilities are not to be understood by analogy with what goes on inside the head, precisely because the ability to use the tools and representations transforms our abilities to complete cognitive tasks.

The cognitive abilities in question are to be explained by the individual learning how to use tools and representational systems. This requires a developmental perspective, for example in language learning, which will then inform cases where the external tools and representations are being actively used in the now as part of a cognitive task. This is a genuine break with the internalist vision of cognition. I will defend cognitive integration against internalist arguments in the next chapter.

3
Defending Cognitive Integration

3.1 Introduction

Recently internalists (Adams and Aizawa 2001, 2007, forthcoming, Rupert 2004, 2007) have mounted a counter-attack on the attempt to redefine the bounds of cognition. Their counter-arguments are aimed at the extended mind framework, but are also relevant to the integrationist framework. Cognitive integration can be defended against the internalist counter arguments of Adams and Aizawa (henceforth A&A), and Rupert and I shall endeavour to show how.

As we saw in the last chapter, the extended mind hypothesis contributes to the radical project of integrating internal and external processes and vehicles, because it provides a way of thinking about the dynamical integration of internal and external vehicles and processes. The internalist criticisms focus only on the external vehicles and processes and ignore their integration with the internal. If integrationists were committed to the claim that external vehicles were made cognitive or mental just because we are causally linked to them, then they would be very weak. Integrationists do not claim this and the internalist criticisms that follow apply only to a weak and traduced version of cognitive integration.

3.2 The "coupling-constitution fallacy"

The first attack centres on the argument that cognitive processes could be constituted by causal couplings, or manipulations of external vehicles. Internalists argue that coupling, or manipulation,

relations are distinct from constitutive relations. A&A (2007) introduce the fallacy as making an external object cognitive by causally connecting it to a cognitive agent.

The coupling of an object X to a cognitive agent does not entail that X is part of the agent's cognitive apparatus. However, the intrinsic nature of X does determine whether or not it is cognitive. The intrinsic nature of pens, paper and other artefacts is not cognitive. The only entities that are intrinsically cognitive are brains. Therefore external artefacts are not part of cognition. Note the assumption of a pre-existing cognitive agent, to whom the artefacts are coupled.

Critics such as A&A (2001, 2007) and Rupert (2004, 2007) take it that cognitive integrationists think that external vehicles are cognitive *because* they are coupled to individuals. They usually cite C&C as committed to such a view. I think that this is a mistake that is rooted in the use of the parity principle to motivate examples of "extended cognition."

As we noted in the previous chapter, the parity principle is supposed to be an intuition pump, a way of overcoming Cartesian prejudices. It is not, in itself, an argument for the extended mind. However, internalists have seized upon the parity principle, attacking a flawed comparative version which schematically can be stated as, if an external process/vehicle X plays a *similar* role to an internal process/vehicle Y (where Y is cognitive), then X is cognitive. I do not think that C&C's version of the parity principle is helpful as currently framed, nor as caricatured by the internalists.

A&A and Rupert's arguments against the manipulation thesis will be shown to be wrong, because they are aimed at the flawed version of the parity principle. However, the manipulation thesis does not depend upon the parity principle. It follows that cognitive integrationists should drop the flawed version of the parity principle as a motivational tool.

3.2.1 Response to the "coupling-constitution fallacy"

The coupling-constitution fallacy is a misunderstanding of the nature of the coupling/manipulation relation as formulated by cognitive integrationists. A&A claim that the causal coupling of X to Y does not make X a part of Y (Adams and Aizawa 2007). The alleged fallacy assumes something like the following picture: an external object/process X is causally coupled to a cognitive agent Y. The Otto example fits this picture: a notebook coupled to a discrete cognitive agent, whereby the notebook becomes part of the memory system of that agent because it is coupled to the agent. Cognitive integrationists should resist this picture. It is a residual form of internalism, because it assumes a discrete, already formed, cognitive agent. And this is precisely the picture we are arguing against. If we accept the picture of a cognitive agent as implementing a discrete cognitive system, before they ever encounter an external vehicle, then we will have accepted the very picture of cognition we set out to reject. This does not fit with the aim of cognitive integration which is to show how internal and external vehicles and processes are integrated in the completion of cognitive tasks (such as remembering the location of MOMA).

For the cognitive integrationist the picture is like this: my *manipulation* of the notebook and my brain processes together constitute a process of remembering. In cases like these, the process of remembering cannot be described exclusively in terms of biological memory or solely in terms of manipulations of external representations, because it is a hybrid process.

Schematically, X is manipulations of the notebook *reciprocally* coupled to Y – neural processes – which together constitute Z, the process of remembering. Once we have this picture, it is easy to see that A&A have distorted the aim of cognitive integration, it is not to show that artefacts get to be part of cognition just because they are causally coupled to a pre-existing cognitive agent. It is to explain why X and Y are so co-ordinated that they together function as Z which causes further behaviour.

Take this analogous example: the input layer of units in a feed-forward neural network is coupled to the hidden layer of units, but nobody thinks that this makes the input layer part of the hidden layer. However, the coupling of the input units to the hidden layer units does make them part of a wider system, the neural network.

Manipulations of external vehicles play a role in completing a cognitive task, as does the processing of internal vehicles – these roles may be different, but they are complementary. The processing of the task is understood in terms of the integration of internal and external processes. Although there will be cases where we will be more like Inga and rely upon biological memories, there will be many cases where we will be more like Otto and recall a memory by manipulating external vehicles (stored in notebooks, or PDA's etc.).

I agree with A&A and Rupert that the hybrid nature of cognition has to be established independently before a project like cognitive integration can be engaged in – I will provide arguments in its favour in Chapters 4 and 5.

A&A and Rupert have misconstrued the nature of the manipulation thesis, assuming that it is simply a case of causal coupling of a pre-existing cognitive agent to an artefact. It is not. It is also not the case that the parity principle is simply a case of similarity between the internal and the external processes. External vehicles and their manipulation may be really quite different from internal ones. It is the co-ordination (or reciprocal coupling) of internal and external processes that together produce behaviour and there may be equivalent cases where the co-ordination of processes is solely internal and still leads to the same ends.

3.3   The intrinsic content condition

A&A stipulate that if a process is to be counted as cognitive it *must* involve at least some intrinsic/non-derived content (2001, 2007). Any cognitive process *must* involve at least some vehicles with intrinsic/non-derived content (henceforth intrinsic). Note that they do not make the strong claim that cognition *must and can only* be the processing of representations with intrinsic content. A&A robustly state that

> Clearly, we mean that if you have a process that involves no intrinsic content, then the condition rules that the process is non-cognitive. (Adams and Aizawa 2007, p. 48)

If we take it that external vehicles do not have intrinsic content, their content is conventionally determined, then it appears that they cannot be cognitive. There is an important difference between brain states that have their contents intrinsically and words and pictures which get their contents through social convention. A&A take it that if you are committed to a representationalist and/or language of thought theory of cognition, then you need a theory of intrinsic content (2001, p. 49), this seems right to me.

Adams and Aizawa (2007) are also very clear that they think that there are mental representations of things like trees, rocks, birds and grass and that there are also mental representations of words, stop signs, warning lights and gas gauges. The mental representations of natural objects are prime cases of intrinsic content. Their contents are fixed by satisfying naturalistic conditions on meaning – as you might find in Fodor's asymmetric dependency account (1990), or Millikan's biosemantic account (1984, 2002) or Dretske's indicator semantics (1988). However, words, stop signs and so on get their contents through social conventions. Does it follow that mental representations of these items have the same conventional contents?

A&A reject this possibility. In Clark's (2005) reply to A&A, he suggests that a mental representation of a diagram of Euler circles has conventional content. A&A make a distinction between Euler circles that have a conventional meaning and images of Euler circles that have their meanings determined by naturalistic conditions. So, convention determines the meaning of Euler circles and the word "dog".

> But that does nothing to show that it is not the satisfaction of some set of naturalistic conditions on non-derived content that get something in the head to have the meanings of "dog", a stop sign, a white flag, and a warning light. (Adams and Aizawa 2007, p. 50)

It follows that the meanings of mental representations and conventional signs converge, even though their meanings have been fixed via different channels – natural and conventional. They allow Clark the latitude to claim that the content of the image of a Euler circle is dependent upon the social convention, but that this convention does not *constitute* the content of the mental image. They say,

> The dependence of meaning of the mental image of intersecting Euler circles on the social contrivance regarding the intersection of Euler circles is just like the dependence of the meaning of a mental representation of a car on the contrivance of a car. Had the car not been invented, there would not have been mental images of cars. (Adams and Aizawa 2007, p. 51)

A&A are telling us that the only difference between a mental image of a tree and a mental image of a car is that the former is of a natural kind and that the latter is of an artefact. The difference in object type does not affect the way that the content of images gets determined. Hence, Clark is wrong to assume that some mental images get their contents determined conventionally. The image of a Euler circle is determined by causal correlation, or function of indication, or whatever, but the Euler circle gets its meaning by some social convention(s).

I think that there is a problem here; the processes that apply to an image of a Euler circle are not the same as the processes that apply to the Euler circle in virtue of its conventionally determined meaning. Think of it like this: the image of a Euler circle gets in my head because of some causal linkage with external Euler circles, grant the internalist this. The inferences that I make that involve Euler circles depend upon the conventions governing the properties and uses of Euler circles; this is something that the image cannot provide. Allow that there are also mental representations of the conventions governing the properties and uses of Euler circles and that this gets in my head because of some causal linkage (asymmetric dependence say) with the outside world. But it is not the causal linkage which determines the content of this representation, the content of the representation *is* the convention. So unless there are mental representations with conventional content, there can be no cognitive processing of Euler circles.

This exchange between Clark and A&A illustrates their attempt to show that internal vehicles of cognition have intrinsic content, but that external vehicles do not. Given this stipulation, internal processing of vehicles with intrinsic content will always be cognitive. External processing of vehicles with conventionally derived content will not. The external vehicles and processes just do not exhibit the mark of the cognitive, but A&A's mark of the cognitive is seriously wanting.

3.3.1 Response to the intrinsic content condition

Let us start with a simple example: A&A think that the image of a dog, qua mental representation in the brain, gets its content according to some naturalistic theory of content such as asymmetric dependence. The word "dog" by contrast gets its content because of social conventions governing linguistic meaning.

There is a problem for A&A here. A&A say that internal cognitive processes cannot apply to conventional representations, they can only apply to images of them. However, as established above, the image of the Euler circle does not have the same content as the Euler circle. This is because the meaning of the Euler circle is dependent upon social conventions, but the content of the image is not determined by social conventions – A&A do not allow that images could have conventionally determined contents. But, as we saw above, internal processes do not apply to the image of a Euler circle in the same way that we directly manipulate the external Euler circle. Therefore, we cannot carry out the same operations on Euler circles in the head that we can by directly manipulating them if we are guided by A&A's stipulation. By A&A's own stipulation they are restricting the cognitive operations that can be carried out on Euler circles – and by extension all representations with socially determined content. If A&A were to concede that cognitive processes can involve vehicles with socially determined content, whether or not they are in the head, then their objection would become otiose.

By A&A's reasoning, cognition that involves representations with intrinsic content is going to be quite limited, but clearly we are not so limited. This is because we have developed external representational schemes and methods for manipulating them. It is odd, if not blindly stubborn, to think that such a large part of our resources required for completing cognitive tasks is not actually a part of our cognitive economy, simply because it involves manipulations of vehicles with conventionally determined content.

There is another problem lurking here for A&A: they might strengthen the stipulation by insisting that the contents of all conventionally determined representations are derived from internal representations with intrinsic content, including sentences of natural language, stop signs and Euler circles (this is the strong version, held by Fodor, for example). This is problematic because the meaning of a Euler circle is not equivalent to an image in someone's head. Take a different example, the mental image of an aardvark is not the sole constituent of my concept of an aardvark. In fact most of the content of my concept of an aardvark will have been fixed by the conventional methods that A&A find anathema. Concepts go beyond what asymmetric dependence or function of indication can offer. Clearly, any thinking I do by applying my concept of aardvark will be cognitive even though the concept is largely conventionally determined. According to the stricter interpretation of A&A's

stipulation, the only genuine thinking that could be done would involve the image!

An obvious sense in which they are different is that images do not have conceptual contents, but then A&A would be forced to admit that representations with intrinsic content do not have the kind of contents that would figure in cognitive processes involving concepts. The image of a dog is not a symbol that can function as a constituent of a sentence in the language of thought. The word "dog", by contrast, can be a constituent of sentences of English. If the only representations in the head with intrinsic content are imagistic, then intracranial cognition will be of an extremely basic kind. Of course, integrationists think that it is precisely for these reasons that external symbol systems such as language and mathematics are required to transform our basic cognitive capacities.

A&A could respond by making internal representations richer entities than images, but then it is hard to see how their contents get determined by something like asymmetric dependence. I fear that if they pursue that line, then their stipulation will disappear in a circular puff of smoke. If sentences of English just are the expression of thoughts, such that the contents of the sentences are the same as the contents of the thoughts, then I do not understand what the possible difference could be between the processing of internal sentences and external sentences that disbars the latter from exhibiting the hallmark of the cognitive. If external sentences just express the contents of internal sentences in a different coding, then the contents of external sentences just are the intrinsic contents of internal sentences. By A&A's own stipulation, the processing of external representations would be cognitive.[1]

Either A&A's intrinsic mental representations will be too rich – too similar to conventional representations – such that the intrinsic – conventional distinction becomes vacuous or they will be too meagre, in which case they will not be of much use in completing cognitive tasks. Either way the intrinsic/derived distinction looks unhelpful.

A&A are left with a dilemma: either intrinsic representations and conventional representations have different meanings, as in the Euler circle case. In virtue of which limitations will have to be placed on the processing that we are capable of. Or, intrinsic representations and conventional representations have the same contents, either because they converge on the same meanings or one is dependent upon the other. In virtue of which there is no interesting distinction to be had for the cognitive case.

If, on the other hand, A&A are making a simple distinction between how the contents of images of natural objects and images of artefacts are about different kinds of things, then the insight is not of great importance to the integrationist.

But what if we took A&A's money as good – that cognition involves vehicles with at least some intrinsic content, could this in any way pose a threat to integrationists? It is quite possible that cognition involves both external representations with "conventional" content and perceptual representations with "intrinsic" content. They might suppose that an internal visual representation of the external object is required for manipulations of that object. But this would just be to say that the entire cognitive process involves some vehicles with intrinsic content and some with conventional content. If things turned out this way it would not harm the integrationist approach at all. The integrationist takes a cognitive practice – manipulations of an external vehicle – to exhibit the mark of the cognitive because it is integrated with internal processes and it is aimed at the completion of a cognitive task.

As we saw above, once we understand the manipulation thesis properly then we know that the coupling constitution fallacy is aimed at the wrong target. When we understand a process as composed of internal and external manipulations, $X + Y$, then the combination of those manipulations, Z, can contain both internal vehicles with intrinsic contents and external vehicles with conventional contents. Therefore, in whatever way you pose the intrinsic content condition, it is no worry for integrationists.

3.4 Extended cognitive science is no science at all

The third attack involves the worry that there is little chance of finding any causal regularities covering both the brain and the arte-facts, such that we might construct a "brain-tool science." Tools, as such, do not constitute a natural kind – DVD players and FM radios, for example, process information differently from one another. It follows that a brain-tool science would have to cover a motley of processes and this could not be the basis of a genuine scientific enterprise.[2]

Take the Otto example (Clark and Chalmers 1998). Otto receives input from the environment, there is an exhibition on at the MOMA, and he then retrieves the location of MOMA from his extended memory system, which causes him, as behavioural output, to go to 53rd street. Inga receives the same input from the environment, retrieves the information from a part of her brain, which then causes her to go to 53rd street.

C&C say that in the case of Otto and Inga there is a sufficient *functional similarity* between Otto's use of his notebook and Inga's recall from biological memory, that we are inclined to say that Otto has beliefs. I take this to mean the following: The functional role that Otto's retrieval of information about the location of MOMA plays in his going to 53rd street is sufficiently similar to the functional role that the pattern of activation in a part of Inga's brain plays in her going to 53rd street that we are inclined to say that Otto has beliefs.

As such the physical implementation of the functional role is irrelevant to the functional level of description. It is a matter of irrelevant implementational detail that Otto's behaviour is caused by his using his notebook and that Inga's is caused by a pattern of activation in her brain. A&A's problem is that Otto could make use of a variety of media to recall the memory that MOMA is on 53rd street, such as notebooks, handheld PC's, CD's and so on. These media do not all work in the same way, which is supposed to lead to a motley of processes and vehicles and no genuine cognitive kinds – hence no real science.

However, I think that the worry trades upon an ambiguity between media and vehicle. For Otto it is the written sentence "MOMA is on 53rd street" that is the vehicle and this is distinct from the medium in which it is implemented – a page of a notebook or the screen of a PDA. The contents of Otto and Inga's beliefs are the same, even if they are accessing different vehicles to retrieve that belief content. Different media may prove to have different properties that affect access time to the contents – it might take Otto longer to retrieve the belief content than Inga for example, but that is a different issue.

A related worry is raised by Rupert (2004, pp. 407–15), who thinks that the Otto model of an extended memory system is not very plausible for understanding the case of the conversation-facilitating role of memory. He claims that in any conversation external vehicles, such as written language in notebooks, are not likely to play much of a role, whereas "internal storage" looks irreplaceable. The case of the "extended conversationalist" would involve the continuous writing down of what has just been said and referring back to it. Rupert claims that conversations are not like this, they depend upon the role of internal working memory. The conclusion Rupert draws is that we should reject the claim that the external processes in the Otto case could be constitutive of working memory; because the nature of the internal processes that make up working memory in the conversational case are so *dissimilar* to the processes in the Otto case. Rupert works with a rather impoverished notion of what could count as external supports in a conversation, and his claim that conversation relies only on internal working memory could be rejected for that reason.

What internalists ought to be arguing for is the claim that internal and external processes differ in *important* and *relevant* respects.[3] A&A think that the important and relevant respect in which they differ is that internal processes involve intrinsic content and external ones do not. It is less clear what the important and relevant differences are for Rupert.

Both A&A and Rupert argue that internal vehicles and processes and external vehicles and processes are dissimilar in important respects. This militates against the claim that the latter could be cognitive. This argument only works if we take the parity principle, as a simple case of similarity, as a primary reason in favour of cognitive integration. However, if we do not consider the parity principle as a primary reason in favour of cognitive integration, then the dissimilarity objection has no force. A proper understanding of the manipulation thesis is required to deflect this internalist objection, as we will see below.

3.4.1   Response to the extended cognitive science is no science at all objection

A&A and Rupert's arguments trade on the claims that internal and external information processing are different and that there is too much variety in the kinds of external information processing. This is because, A&A and Rupert think that if they can show that internal vehicles and processes are different from external vehicles and processes, then it follows that external vehicles and processes are not cognitive. I think that cognitive integrationists should accept the antecedent but deny that the consequent follows.

They should accept the first claim because it is a mistake to think of cognitive integration as just externalising what is already in the head – the parity principle is apt to lead us in this direction:

> They [C&C] contend that the active causal processes that extend into the environment *are just like the ones found in intracranial cognition*. (Adams and Aizawa 2001, p. 56).

Rupert (2004) makes precisely the same mistake; he clearly thinks that the downfall of cognitive integration is its attempt to show that external vehicles and processes are like internal ones:

> My strategy is to focus on a specific kind of cognitive state, memory, and here the thrust of the discussion is twofold: I argue that the external portions of extended "memory" states (processes) differ so greatly from internal memories (the process of remembering) that they should be treated as distinct kinds; this quells *any temptation to argue for HEC* [hypothesis of extended cognition] *from brute analogy (namely, extended cognitive states are like wholly internal ones; therefore, they are of the same explanatory cognitive kind; therefore there are extended cognitive states)*. (Rupert 2004, p. 407) (My italics)

However, cognitive integrationists who do not rely on the parity principle clearly avoid this criticism, because they take the manipulation thesis and the thesis of hybrid cognition to be the primary motivation for cognitive integration.

> Instead, it [working memory] must be viewed as essentially *hybrid*, made up of two distinct components. In particular, the processes involved in working memory must be viewed as made up of both biological processes *and* processes of external manipulation of relevant information-bearing structures in the environment. (Rowlands 1999, p. 147)

> Remembering, on this view, involves exploiting internal, bodily, and environmental resources in order to produce some sort of action, often social in nature. (Wilson 2004, p. 191)

There is nothing in the definition of working memory that Rupert chooses to work with that precludes the integrationist account: working memory is part of "an integrated system for holding and manipulating information during the performance of complex cognitive tasks" (Baddeley 2000, p. 78). Since it is precisely because internal and external components are integrated that they allow information to be available for the completion of cognitive tasks. But Rupert thinks that because he can show that internal memory functions differently to external memory, he has undermined the whole cognitive integrationist project.

However, this can only be the case if cognitive integrationists proceed by showing that external processes involved in remembering get to be counted as *memory* because they are sufficiently similar to internal processes involved in remembering. The argument fails if we jettison the flawed version of the parity principle. Rowlands' and Wilson's accounts of the integration of internal and external memory fall quite happily under Rupert's chosen definition of working memory.

If that line of attack is blocked, then Rupert could take each case on its merits. This he does with some success in the case of the role of memory in conversation. It seems likely that we follow conversations by drawing heavily on internal resources, but there are other cases of memory where we draw heavily on external resources. Assume agreement with those psychologists cited by Rupert, why does it follow that all of memory is like the case of following a conversation? If all memory is internal in the way Rupert describes, then why is it easy for us to follow a conversation, but not so easy to recall the relevant detail at a later date? Why is it difficult to remember long strings of mathematical equations? Why do we need maps? We may not use many environmental cues in following a conversation, but we definitely use environmental cues in finding our way about. In these cases we do not need an explicit model in the head, sometimes the environment serves as its own best representation, or the representation in question is already in the environment – a map, for example.

It is important to cognitive integration that external manipulations do something different to brain processes. In the head, there are connectionist vehicles and processes over them. There is not anything in the environment that looks like connectionist vehicles and processes over them. There are symbols, such as diagrams and linguistically structured vehicles, and their manipulation is different from manipulations of connectionist vehicles – just think of the Euler circle case.

Otto's use of his notebook is cognitive because he manipulates the vehicles (sentences) in his book to complete a cognitive task. Inga completes the cognitive task using only her biological resources. Otto's manipulation of external vehicles is not cognitive because it is similar to Inga's biological memory, but because Otto and his notebook constitute "an integrated system for holding and manipulating information during the performance of complex cognitive tasks" (Baddeley 2000, p. 78).

This move requires us to take seriously the complementarity of the internal and external cognitive resources necessary for their integration. There is a complementarity between what the biological brain can do and what the environment provides, such that inner processes and vehicles and outer processes and vehicles work together to complete a cognitive task (Clark 2001a, 2003, Sutton 2007). We must also take into account the transformatory impact this integration has on our cognitive capacities, both in the here and now and during cognitive development. On this view the external cognitive environment transforms what the individual can do cognitively, both synchronically and diachronically (Vygotsky 1978, Wertsch, 1985).

So the processing of internal and external vehicles, whilst different, is complementary and as integrationists we should try to show how they are complementary.

However, it does not follow from this that external manipulations are a motley of processes. For example, there is an interesting difference between the Tetris case and the Otto case. In the Tetris case an epistemic action is performed in the place of an internal representation. In the case of Otto, an external representation is used instead of an internal one. But Otto must have learnt to manipulate the notebook as a repository of representations, such that Otto's bodily processes and his manipulation of the representations in the notebook constitute his act of remembering. Similarly, Tetris players learn to manipulate directly the differently shaped blocks, rather than rotate images of them in their heads. There is nothing particularly "motley" here, just two different kinds of manipulation that both allow for the completion of cognitive tasks.

A&A and Rupert miss the point here; certainly DVD's process "information" differently from brains, but it does not follow from this that cognitive integration is false. When we manipulate external vehicles, we are not doing what DVD players do! There are, as pointed out in the introduction to this book, various types of manipulation:

1. Biological cases of coupling such as extended phenotypes and animate vision (biological coupling).
2. Using the environment as its own representation, obviating the need for internal representations, as in Tetris (epistemic actions).
3. The use of language and external props to direct and structure practical actions in completing tasks (self-correcting actions).
4. And most importantly, manipulations of external representational and notational systems according to certain normative practices, as in mathematics (cognitive practices).

There is nothing motley about these three classes of manipulation, what unifies them is that they *are* cases of manipulations of external vehicles. Cognitive integrationists need to make these distinct cases clear, but once they are clear, the internalist's arguments fail.

3.5   Conclusion

Cognitive integration makes sense when we understand it as not just externalising what is already in the head. The manipulation of external vehicles is importantly different from manipulations of internal vehicles and their integration is the unit of cognitive analysis. We are not just coupling artefacts to pre-existing cognitive agents; the organism becomes a cognitive agent by being coupled to the external environment. Explaining this integration of the internal and the external involves both a dynamical account of the reciprocal causal interaction between internal and external vehicles and processes and an account of how we learn to manipulate external vehicles in accordance with relevant cognitive norms. Hence, the extended mind hypothesis contributes to the wider project of integrating the internal and the external because it focuses on the dynamical account of causal coupling. Cognitive integration goes further than the extended mind hypothesis, because it explains how external cognitive vehicles are manipulated in a wider context where cognitive practices allow us to complete cognitive tasks.

I shall now begin the task of formulating cognitive integration in the final four chapters.

4
Cognitive Integration: Embodied Engagements and the Manipulation Thesis

> We may...be said to *know how* by means of our habits ...We walk and read aloud, we get off and on street cars, we dress and undress, and do a thousand useful acts without thinking of them. We *know* something, namely, *how* to do them.
>
> – John Dewey

> Let me explain in terms of the martial arts. As a beginner you know nothing of stance or sword position, so you have nothing to dwell on in yourself mentally. If someone strikes at you, you just fight, without thinking of anything. Then when you learn various things like stance, how to wield a sword, where to place the attention, and so on, your mind lingers on various points, so you find yourself all tangled up when you try to strike. But if you practice day after day and month after month, eventually stance and swordplay don't hang on your mind anymore, and you are like a beginner who knows nothing.... The cogitating side of your brain will vanish and you will come to rest in a state where there is no concern.
>
> – Takuan (16th century)

4.1 Introduction

It is through our bodies that we primarily engage with the world and through this engagement the body is constantly integrating with the environment. When body and environment co-ordinate, the environment becomes part of the resources the organism has for acting, thinking or communicating. How, though, ought we to understand the co-ordination, or reciprocal coupling, of body and environment as accomplishing thinking? Reciprocal coupling is a symmetrical relation, the organism manipulates its environment in one direction, but the result of this environmental alteration feeds back to the organism prompting further bodily actions. Our focus in this chapter is on the nature of bodily manipulations. There are two ways to understand manipulations that I want to explore.

First, there are the body schemas and motor programmes (collections of body schemas) that are completed as bodily manipulations of the environment. Some of these will be innate, such as swallowing, and some learned such as writing, or driving a car. Body schemas are the embodied forms of manipulations.

Secondly, there are the environmental norms which govern these manipulations and that are followed in training and action (the first consciously, the second not). The co-ordination of body and environment as accomplishing cognition or thought is, therefore, governed both by body schemas and by biological and cultural norms. These will draw on many learned skills and habits, which will have been inculcated through body images as conscious rehearsal and practice. This is also a way in for us to understand manipulations as embodied practices and as governed by cognitive norms (I shall elaborate this idea in Chapter 6). It is also why a Vygotskyan developmental account of the bodily and cultural bases of cognition and thought will demonstrate the ways in which body and environment come to be integrated through training, education and general enculturation (in Chapter 7).

In this chapter, I shall focus on the first way to understand the co-ordination between body and environment and begin to connect it up with the second through the manipulation thesis. The first section outlines the notion of body schema and how body schemas become integrated with the environment. Then I shall move on to outline the manipulation thesis and explain the different types of manipulation through examples.

4.2 Embodied engagements

Gallagher (2005) has done us the great service of clarifying the concepts of body image and body schema respectively. A body image "consists of a system of perceptions, attitudes, and beliefs pertaining to one's own body" (2005, p. 24). A body schema is "a system of sensory-motor capacities that function without awareness or the necessity of perceptual monitoring" (2005, p. 24).

> So the difference between body image and body schema is like the difference between a *perception* (or conscious monitoring) of movement and the actual *accomplishment* of one's own movement . . . (2005, p. 24)

I want to concentrate on the body schema. They are subpersonal processes that dynamically govern posture and movement, and Gallagher claims they do this in a *close* to automatic way (Gallagher 2005, p. 26). They are only *close* to automatic, because body schemas can be part of a goal-directed activity, such as catching a ball in a game of cricket. There are higher level goals and intentions involved in this action, but our consciousness is not directed at the movements of our body, but at the ball. Hence, we are not aware of the functions of the body schema in governing our posture and movement, in so far as these are part of a goal-directed activity.

By contrast when I am learning some skilled activity, I often will attend to awareness of my posture and movement. I might be consciously monitoring my grip whilst holding a racquet or bat, trying to get "the feel right." I might try to imitate the movements of those more expert than myself. However, as Gallagher reminds us,

> Even in such cases the contribution made to the control of movement by my perceptual awareness of my body will always find its complement in capacities that are defined by the operations of a body schema that continues to function to maintain balance and movement. (Gallagher 2005, p. 27)

Repertoires of body schemas function together as motor programmes (Gallagher 2005). Some motor programmes are learned such as riding a bike and writing and some are innate such as swallowing. What is important about schemas and motor programmes is that they can exhibit a high degree of integration with the environment. In these cases the body schema incorporates parts of the environment that are not incorporated into the body image, such as the hammer in the carpenter's hand (Gallagher 2005, p. 37).

The integration has a phenomenological aspect, where a part of the environment can feel like an extension to the body, in these cases the body schema goes beyond the narrow boundary that is apparent from the body image. It also has a neural aspect:

> This extension of the body schema into its surrounding environment is reflected in its neural representations. Not only do bimodal premotor, parietal, and putaminal neuronal areas that represent a given limb or body area also respond to visual stimulation in the environmental space nearby, for some of these neurons the visual receptive field remains "anchored" to the body part when it moves (Fogassi *et al.* 1996; Graziano and Gross 1998; Graziano and Gross 1994). (Gallagher 2005, p. 37)

Motor programmes do not just initiate behaviour they are fully integrated with the environment, and they are constrained by the environment because they often require the perceptual navigation of the environment and the manipulation of environmental objects. Therefore, my body shapes itself to meet the environment, to hold a glass in hand or grip a pencil between fingers and thumb for writing. Body schemas are attuned to environmental affordances for action (Gibson 1979), the glass affords drinking and the pencil writing.

It is in the fluid manipulation of objects in the environment and in fluent skilled activities that we are most likely to find the unconscious integration of the body schema with the environment. Experienced drivers will understand the nature of this integration which involves the seamless co-ordination of body and car, sometimes to such an extent that one cannot recall the details of the journey when the destination is reached (Gallagher 2005). Although the body image involves conscious experience of our own bodies and that experience is of a bounded body, the body schema has no such boundary, it directs our primary embodied engagements with the world and it is because of this that we feel ourselves to be both in and part of the world. Furthermore, it is constitutive of our first cognitive engagements with the world, our perceptual navigation, our imitation of others and our manipulation of the environment.

4.2.1 Expertise

The kinds of expert skilled activities that Dreyfus and Dreyfus (1986) have outlined are clear examples of the integration of body schema and environment. Dreyfus's well-known five stage account of expertise begins with the novice stage of development with its typical reliance upon strict adherence to rules. Tasks are broken down into context-free features that can be recognised without prior experience and familiarity with situations. The transition from novice to competence and proficiency to genuine expertise involves the move from reliance on explicit rules and conscious deliberation to a situation-specific perception and a flexible, adaptive responsiveness to the situation.

Experts often do not need to detach themselves from the situation to analyse it or deliberate about it, they are able to respond fluently and adaptively. The expert is not simply using the same rules that the novice and beginner are consciously dependent upon at a much faster rate. Rather, the expert has the ability to perceive the relevant features of the situation quickly and selectively. This recognition of patterns is directly tied to action, there is no need for an intermediate step of conscious deliberation; "an expert's skill has become so much a part of him that he need be no more aware of it than he is of his own body" (Dreyfus and Dreyfus 1986, p. 30).

4.2.2 A sporting example

This level of expertise is the aim of all professional sports people. John Sutton (Sutton, forthcoming) gives a fascinating analysis of the role of habit and memory in the skilled performance of a cricket batsman.[1] In cricket the batsman deploys what Sutton calls an "open skill," one where the actions of the batsman require a high degree of adaptability to a changing environment. This kind of dynamical and adaptable skill requires a combination of features nicely illustrated by the following quote from Bartlett:

> Suppose I am making a stroke in a quick game, such as tennis or cricket... When I make the stroke I do not, as a matter of fact, produce something absolutely new, and I never merely repeat something old. The stroke is literally manufactured out of the living visual and postural "schemata" of the movement and their interrelations. (Bartlett 1932, 201*f*, also quoted in Sutton, forthcoming)

Developing the relevant motor programmes involves a lot of training in technique and practice of technique in controlled circumstances. The point of this training is to develop the motor programmes (or habit in ordinary language) such that the batsman can respond fluently and adaptively to the current situation in the match.[2] This is a precise example of the integration of body schema with environment and of how body schemas are in part shaped by cultural norms, such as the rules of cricket and the instructions for successfully carrying out a technique. It is not simply a case of a physiological response to the environment.

> When in the context of a game I jump to catch a ball, that action cannot be fully explained by the physiological activity of my body. The pragmatic concern of playing the game motivates the action. The physical environment, the size and shape of the ball, along with the effects of all my previous practice (or lack thereof), and even the rules of the game as they are habitually expressed in the practiced movements of my body, may define how I jump to make a catch. Without a certain amount of selectivity, built up by practice and the cultivation of habitual movements, the body might move in any one of multiple ways, since the possibilities allowed by physiology are much greater than the particular movements necessary to catch the ball in the proper way. Thus the body schema is much more selectively attuned to its environment than what physiology on its own will specify.[3] (Gallagher 2005, 143)

The expert's ability to perceive and flexibly respond to a situation is tied to a well-trained and practiced suite of unconscious body schemas, which function best without the intrusion of conscious deliberative thought, or even a series of intermediate subpersonal processes on representations.

Returning to the nature of expertise, professional sportspeople report just this aim in their constant and dedicated practising. The Australian cricket captain Warwick Armstrong described batting practice as leading to a state "when we are unconscious of any hesitation at all, acting as if by instinct; for the occasion prompts the action. Then we play naturally; that is we have made habit second nature" (Armstrong, 1922, p. 47, quoted in Sutton forthcoming). The English batsman Ken Barrington describes this state in the following terms "... when you're playing well you don't think about *anything*." He also describes the opposite state in the following terms, "When you're out of form you're conscious of needing to do things right, so you have to think first and act second. To make runs under those conditions is mighty difficult" (Both quotes from Barrington 1968, pp. 97–8, quoted in Sutton forthcoming).

However, the Dreyfusian notion of expertise and the professional sportsperson's search for *flow* through perfection of technique is not the whole story to habitual skilled activity. John Sutton introduces the notion of an "instructional nudge," a conscious verbal cue, which in cricket might be "watch the ball" or "play each ball on its merits." Using language to control, structure, and sometimes re-orient our actions is a case of what I call a self-correcting action (see the next section). Such "nudges" can be used to cue in the right motor programmes, rather than as conscious efforts to move in the right way.

This leads us nicely into a discussion of the manipulation thesis, where we will encounter a variety of manipulations some tending towards fluent, unconscious Dreyfusian expertise and some involving the direct intrusion of conscious thought in language and sometimes to re-orient ourselves to a task, or structure and direct our activity. Then there is the case of manipulating external representations.

4.3 The manipulation thesis

In an early formulation of the manipulation thesis, Mark Rowlands highlights the locational and constitutive aspects of bodily manipulations:

> [C]ognitive processes are not located exclusively in the skin of cognising organisms because such processes are, in part, made up of physical or bodily *manipulation* of structures in the environments of such organisms. (Rowlands 1999, p. 23)

Cognitive processes are not exclusively located in the body and this is underwritten by a constitutive claim that cognitive processes are, in part, constituted by the bodily manipulation of structures in the environment. The locational and constitutive claims are to be cashed out in terms of the crucial role played by dynamics in understanding the causal relation between agents and environments, known as reciprocal coupling (as we saw in the first part of the book). Reciprocal coupling also has to be taken in conjunction with the role of external representations, or vehicles, in the completion of cognitive tasks.

This early formulation of the manipulation thesis and the role of reciprocal coupling as found in active externalism are insufficient on their own. The manipulation thesis as a constituent thesis of cognitive integration is first understood to be an embodied engagement with the world, as we saw in the first sections of this chapter. Secondly it is not simply a causal relation, bodily manipulations are also normative – they are embodied practices developed through habit and training and governed by cognitive norms. In the rest of this chapter, I will outline four different classes of bodily manipulation of the environment and look at some examples of the first two classes. The third and fourth classes will be dealt with in greater detail in Chapters 6 and 7. Finally, I will introduce the Peircean Principle as an account of representation that is agnostic about the location of representations, in preparation for the next two chapters.

We can identify at least four classes of manipulation:

1. *Biological coupling* – such as extended phenotypes, animate vision.
2. *Epistemic Actions* – using the environment as its own representation, obviating the need for internal representations (as in Tetris).
3. *Self–Correcting Actions* – The use of language and exogenous props to direct and structure practical actions in completing tasks.
4. *Cognitive Practices* – manipulations of external representational and notational systems regulated by cognitive norms (as in mathematics).

Examples of biological coupling run from non-cognitive cases such as phonotaxis in crickets (Webb 1994) and bee dances (Millikan 1993, 2002) (see the next chapter for a comprehensive account of these) up to sensorimotor contingencies (O'Regan and Noë 2001) and animate vision (Ballard 1991).

Kirsh and Maglio (1994) have dubbed the second class of manipulations epistemic actions. An epistemic action involves directly manipulating the environment to bring about a better state in a problem solving/planning task, rather than constructing an internal representation and manipulating that.[4]

An example of a self-correcting action is the role of spoken language in structuring activity, such as Sutton's instructional nudges. In these kinds of cases, we use speech as a corrective tool.

The classic example of a cognitive practice is Rumelhart and McClelland's (1986) example of using pen and paper to complete a mathematical algorithm. Performing long multiplication involves mastery over a notational system, which involves cognitive norms for manipulating those notations when completing cognitive tasks.

By the end of this chapter, we will be in a position to understand what the manipulation thesis is and what it actually entails. This is important because the bodily manipulation of the environment is the central strand of cognitive integration. Hence, it is rather crucial to understand just what it entails – that it involves embodied engagements with the world, we have already seen, that some of these embodied engagements are cognitive and that they are normative has yet to be fully explored. Both the hybrid mind thesis and the cognitive practice thesis, the topics of the next two chapters, require a robust notion of manipulation.

Furthermore, as we saw in the last chapter, critics of extended mind arguments show a distinct misunderstanding of what the manipulation thesis is (Adams and Aizawa 2001, 2007, Rupert 2004). They tend to focus on a flawed version of the parity principle[5] and an overly simplistic conception of reciprocal coupling.

4.3.1 Biological coupling

I shall look at cases of biological coupling in detail in the next chapter, including the evolutionary reasons for organism–environment systems and the continuity of these cases with cognitive ones. The body schema is a primary example of biological coupling, a visceral bodily engagement with the world. An example of this kind of biological coupling which provides an embodied approach to perception is the enactive or sensorimotor contingency approach (Noë 2004).

O'Regan and Noë (2001, p. 390) define their approach to perception as, "vision is a mode of exploration of the world that is mediated by knowledge of what we call sensorimotor contingencies." The experience of the visual world is not explained by internal representations of it – this conclusion is also reached by Yarbus (1967), Ballard

(1991), Churchland Ramachandran and Sejnowski (1994). Instead visual experiences are dependent upon the organism exploring its environment and by mastery of sensorimotor contingencies. Mastery of the contingencies is cashed out in terms of the extraction of law-like regularities that pertain to the way that motor activity results in changes to sensory input.

When moving towards an object it will begin to dominate your visual field. In moving around it, you change the profile of the object – front, side, back and so on. (Myin and O'Regan 2002). It is in this way that visual perception and movement are reciprocally coupled. Your visual perception and ability to move around your environment is dependent upon patterns of sensorimotor contingency. Therefore, when you see an object, seeing it consists in eye movements coupled to bodily movements as patterns of sensorimotor contingency.

One way of interpreting this enactive account of perception is to think of perception as being a skill (Clark 2000b). If perception is a skill, then visual sensations are not caused by some internal process in the brain, rather they are constituted by a set of capacities of the organism to act. The skill theory gets us to focus on the activity of an organism in an environment. We then turn away from the traditional focus on perception as building a detailed inner representation of the external world. The reciprocal coupling of the organism to its environment becomes the focus of theories of perception and not the construction of internal representations (Menary 2006b).

Biological manipulations show that we, as biological organisms, are already attuned to reciprocal coupling with the environment. These cases demonstrate that we are embodied and situated and that we use the strategy of directly manipulating the environment where the world is its own best model. In this chapter and the next, I will also show that biological manipulation can involve manipulations of biological representations, which have normative conditions for their repeatability. There is, then, a biological precedent for manipulations of external representations. The next case of manipulation is epistemic actions. They are a step up from biological manipulations towards cognitive practices.

4.3.2   Epistemic action

Epistemic actions are an example of Brooks's slogan that the world is its own best model. As with biological coupling, epistemic actions involve a tight coupling between body and world. We can make a distinction between epistemic actions and cognitive practices, where epistemic actions involve directly interacting with the environment without the need for internal representations. However, there may well be cases where the two types of manipulation are combined in the joint completion of a cognitive task – I shall look at such an example later.

However, over-reliance on cases of epistemic action to make the case for the manipulation thesis can fall into the hands of the cognitive internalist. This is because the usual motivation for appealing to epistemic actions is to "off-load" cognitive complexity onto the environment, thereby making a cognitive task more tractable and this can be given a "trivial" explanation. The trivial reading is that re-organising the environment so as to make it more easily processed by internal resources is an intelligent strategy but does not indicate that such activities are themselves part of the processing of a cognitive task.

The integrationist needs to counter this "trivialising" strategy by showing how epistemic actions are part of a process of continuous reciprocal coupling between environment, body and brain, which together constitute the processing necessary for the completion of a cognitive task. I will argue for this by reference to the work of Kirsh and Maglio on epistemic actions.

Kirsh and Maglio, henceforth K&M (1994), are interested in a class of actions which they call epistemic actions, which make mental computation[6] "easier, faster, or more reliable" (1994, p. 513). These are external physical actions which the agent performs in order to alter their own computational state. They wish to shift the emphasis from planning and choosing an action so as to achieve a goal to performing actions which simplify the computation required to achieve that goal. Instead of thinking of an agent computing various plans and choosing an action which will most efficiently bring about the desired goal, K&M want us to think of agents directly manipulating their environment so as to reduce the need for such internal computation.

Their main line of interest is how epistemic actions reduce computational workload for "tasks requiring agents to react quickly" (Kirsh and Maglio 1994, p. 514). K&M put the emphasis on epistemic action as merely simplifying computation, or making things easier and quicker. On page 514, they say,

We use the term epistemic action to designate a physical action whose primary function is to improve cognition by:

1. Reducing the memory involved in mental computation, that is, space complexity.
2. Reducing the number of steps involved in mental computation, that is, time complexity.
3. Reducing the probability of error of mental computation, that is, unreliability.

So far they seem to be providing fodder for the internalist's worry, but I shall put this worry to rest soon. Before doing so I turn to their example of epistemic action – the game Tetris. In the game, falling geometric shapes have to be directed to available slots in a continually emerging structure. A rotation button can be used to orient the shapes relative to the slots – so that discrimination of fit can be judged. K&M say,

> the clearest reason to doubt that deciding where to place a zoid involves mental rotation is that zoids can be *physically* rotated 90 degrees in as few as 100 ms. whereas we estimate that it takes in the neighbourhood of 800 to 1200 ms to mentally rotate a zoid 90 degrees. (Kirsh and Maglio 1994, p. 514)

Even allowing for an extra 200 ms for subjects to select the rotate button, the time-saving benefits of physical over mental rotation are obvious. They go on to say that time is not the only benefit. The cost on working memory and attention to produce and sustain mental images of zoids would harm performance – physically rotating the zoid is computationally less demanding than mental rotation.

Of course, manipulations and computations do not have to be seen in such a dichotomous fashion. Manipulations restructure the environment in such a way that it is easier to process, but it is unclear why that restructuring of the environment is not itself part of the computation (an external part). It is clear that such restructuring is not part of the computation if all the computation and computational states are in the head, but this is the very position which we are questioning and investigating. Whether or not epistemic actions are part of the computation depends, partly, upon how seriously we take K&M's distinction between epistemic and pragmatic actions.

> Let us call actions whose primary function is to bring the agent closer to his or her physical goal pragmatic actions, to distinguish them from epistemic actions. (Kirsh and Maglio 1994, p. 515)

The distinction is more interestingly illustrated a few paragraphs on

> one significant consequence of recognizing epistemic action as a category of activity is that if we continue to view planning as state space search, we must redefine the state space in which planning occurs. That is, instead of interpreting the nodes of a state space graph to be physical states, we have to interpret them as representing both physical and informational states. (Kirsh and Maglio 1994, p. 515)

Classically we might think of a plan and actions which implement the plan as distinct; however, K&M's point is that epistemic actions are part of strategy creation and problem solving. Clearly, problem solving is cognitive. So if epistemic actions are part of that problem-solving process, and not merely the result of problem solving or the physical means by which plans are implemented, then we have a very good reason for claiming that epistemic actions are part of the problem-solving process. Accepting this depends upon taking seriously the distinction between epistemic and pragmatic action and seeing a tighter coupling between external epistemic actions and internal computations.

K&M themselves say of their approach that, "its chief novelty lies in allowing individual functional units inside the agent to be in closed-loop interaction with the outside world" (Kirsh and Maglio 1994, p. 542). They go on to talk of "a tighter coupling between internal and external *processes*." And later,

> This way of thinking treats the agent as having a more *cooperative* and interactional relation with the world: the agent both adapts to the world as found and changes the world, not just pragmatically, which is a first order change, but epistemically, so that the world becomes a place that is easier to adapt to. Consequently we expect

that a well adapted agent ought to know how to strike a balance between internal and *external* computation. It ought to achieve an appropriate level of cooperation between internal organizing processes and *external organizing processes* so that, in the long run, less work is performed. (Kirsh and Maglio 1994, p. 546)

K&M are here talking about the kind of coupling which integration-ists are after because the external processes, epistemic actions, are coupled to internal processes – such as working memory and atten-tion. All components are causally active and they jointly govern beha-viour, because epistemic action plus internal computation jointly govern pragmatic action. This way of thinking has had a profound influence on the development of extended mind style arguments (Clark and Chalmers 1998).

K&M give us a way of thinking about the role of action such that we can unify physical space and information-processing space. The distinction between a realm of internal computations upon inputted information and a realm of outputted physical behaviours must be rejected. The information-processing space includes both computa-tional processes in the head and computational processes outside of the head. Clark has a nice analogy here:

Einstein replaced the independent notions of space and time with a unified construct (spacetime), Kirsh and Maglio suggest that cognitive science may need to replace the independent constructs of physical space and information processing space with a unified physico-informational space. (Clark 1997, p. 66)

Epistemic actions and computations take place within the same state space. If this state space is the problem-solving state space, then we have difficulty in pulling apart mind, action and world in such a neat fashion – especially given the dynamical conception of a state space above.

However, the internalist thinks that there is an easy way of demon-strating how this division works: the only restructuring of the envir-onment which is relevant to the problem solving/planning agent occurs inside the agent's head. In other words,

> The structure of the environment which matters to cognition is the structure the agent represents (or at least presupposes in the way it manipulates its representations). (Kirsh and Maglio 1994, p. 545)

If all the relevant structure is in the head, this obviates the need for epistemic action, where the world is structured in such a way as to negate the need for structured representations in the head.

But K&M have established that there is such a class of actions as epistemic actions and now the internalist is at a loss to account for them. If we were to agree with the internalist that all the relevant structure, all the computational states and processes are in the head, then we cannot explain the performance of Tetris players. If we explain their performance by making reference to external manipulations as part of their cognitive processing (the problem-solving), then we can explain their performance. The trivialising strategy is blocked by the inability to explain the Tetris player's performance by internal cognitive resources alone. The internalist is forced into this position because of the difference between epistemic actions and pragmatic actions – epistemic actions are aimed at making a move in the problem-solving state space, pragmatic actions are not.[7]

The expert Tetris players in K&M's study have developed motor programmes for manipulating the buttons that transform the zoids on the screen. They will have started by conscious rehearsal of rules which would guide their manipulations. As experts their fluent and fluid dependence upon well-trained body schemas no longer requires direct conscious application of rules. Note, though, that the manipulation of the buttons is itself a normative practice, something that is learned and habitualised. It is not simply a case of reciprocal coupling, although it involves this.

K&M's focus is on epistemic actions as interactions with the environment where an internal representation is not required. This is encapsulated in Brooks's slogan "the world is its own best model." We saw the same kind of strategy in sensorimotor accounts of perception, in the previous section. It has a biological basis in the reciprocal coupling of an organism to its environment. These are the first two prongs of the manipulation thesis; many complex cognitive behaviours arise without the need for the processing of internal representations, because we can always manipulate the environment instead.

As we have seen, cognitive internalists often try to shrug off biological coupling and epistemic actions as trivial; they are just cases of off-loading cognitive complexity onto the environment. This trivialising strategy finds some evidence in the following kind of rhetoric:

> A complementary strategy can be defined as any organising activity which recruits external elements to reduce cognitive loads. The external elements can be our fingers or hands, pencil and paper, movable icons, counters, measuring devices, or other entities in our immediate environment. Typical organising activities include pointing, arranging the position and orientation of nearby objects (Kirsh, 95), writing things down, manipulating counters, rulers or other artefacts that can encode the state of a process or simplify perception. (Kirsh 1995b, p. 212)

It provides fodder for the internalist intuition that cognition is in the head, but that there are certain props and heuristic strategies which we use to lighten the cognitive burden. This is why internalists such as Adams and Aizawa (2001, 2007) find the extended mind so odd, they cannot see why anyone would count these external props and heuristics as part of cognition. Cognitive integrationists should avoid this pitfall by locating epistemic actions in the problem-solving state space, not just as a clever strategy for off-loading complexity onto the environment. Biological coupling and epistemic actions show that interaction with the environment replaces the need for the processing of internal representations of the environment; nonetheless these classes of manipulations are still part of our cognitive economy.

We have already seen an example of self-correcting actions earlier in this chapter and we shall look at another in Chapter 7. The fourth class of manipulation, and in my view the more important, is manipulations of external representations (cognitive practices) where the special properties of external representations and their manipulation transform our cognitive abilities. Cognitive practices are different from the first two classes of manipulation in some important respects. First, the cognitive agent must master the cognitive norms for manipulating the representations. Secondly, the basic cognitive resources of the brain are transformed by becoming coupled to external representational systems. The integrationist account of systematicity (see Chapter 6) shows precisely how this works.

To illustrate the differences here, take the following examples of epistemic actions from Kirsh (1995a, 1995b):

- While searching for an appropriate jigsaw piece in solving a jigsaw puzzle, players tend to construct groupings such as corner pieces, edge pieces, same colour, similar shape. These intermediate steps aid visual search, but their function is cognitive or epistemic, in that they do not actually bring players physically closer to their pragmatic goals.
- When setting out to organize a bookshelf according to subject heading, the sort routine often followed involves distributing books first on the floor in different regions over the bookshelf, as if to prove that a particular subject arrangement makes sense. These interim steps frequently require revision: their function is as much cognitive or epistemic as practical, since the early arrangement of books may not find their way into the final arrangement.
- When playing Tetris, players have little time to choose their target placement, yet they rotate pieces often four or five times more than necessary. This extra rotation is not evidence of flailing, but rather plays a functional role in their computation of their goal placement.
- In solving cryptarithmetic problems subjects often mutter, write down intermediate conjectures, partial results, re-write elements in different places on their scrap page. These actions seem to help problem solving, although it is not always evident how.
- In solving simple geometry problems, subjects try out a range of different constructions. The function of constructions is not necessarily to permit solution directly, but often to make certain properties of the structure more explicit, or to prompt the agent to notice similarities between this problem and others seen before.

The first three examples involve re-organising the physical layout of the environment so as to more easily complete a cognitive task. The last two involve manipulating external representations to complete a cognitive task. They are not the same class of manipulation, the second class involves mastery over a representational or notational system.

However, there may be cases where epistemic action and manipulations of external representations are blended to some degree. King Beach of the City University of New York produced a study (Beach 1988) of how expert bartenders are able to remember long lists of drink orders given to them by patrons. When you go to the bar with an unfortunately long list of drinks, you might rehearse them in your head, or out loud, so as not to forget them. Is this what expert bartenders do when presented with your long list of drinks? In Beach's experiment, four drinks orders were orally presented to the bartender, who then made the drinks as quickly and accurately as possible. Performance was measured in terms of speed and accuracy. The task was given to 10 novice bartenders and 10 expert bartenders. In the first trial the bartenders had to cope with the additional hindrance of counting backwards from 40 by threes, to interfere with their ability to mentally rehearse the orders. The novices made many errors, but the experts were unaffected by the additional task of counting backwards.

The second experiment cleverly revealed the difference between novice and expert. All the subjects were forced to use identically proportioned opaque black glasses as opposed to standard glassware. Novices were unaffected by this change, but the experts increased their errors by 17-fold. The experts were using the type of glass selected for the drink and the positioning of those glasses close to the type of drink, as they were being ordered, as a type of interactive external memory. Unlike the novices who were trying to memorise a list and then remember where the glasses and drinks were. Once the expert bartenders were no longer allowed to interact with their environment in the right way, their performance fell.

Now, although Beach's interpretation of the use of the "bar environment" by the Bartenders is in terms of a "mere" aid to memory, there is a lot more going on in the construction and manipulation of the mnemonic bar. The configuration of physical objects in the bar allows the bartender to interact with glasses and drinks in certain normative ways. For example, the location of beer glasses near to beer pumps allows the bartender to place a beer glass next to the right beer pump as the drink is ordered. The beer glass acts as a representational marker of what was ordered, beer, its spatial proximity to the beer pump is a sign of which beer has been ordered and so on for wine glasses etc.

This interaction of the bartender with the environment acts as an efficient external memory store for drinks orders. The bartender must interact with the environment, in terms of the configuration of objects, glasses and pumps, and must recognise the difference between beer glasses, wine glasses, whisky tumblers and so on. They must recognise the representational significance of glass type and spatial position; they cannot do this if all the glasses look exactly the same. The "mnemonic bar environment" is a representational system, involving objects and the configuration of those objects, which the Bartender does not need in his head. The structure of the mnemonic bar allows the expert bartender to perform the relevant epistemic actions. However, the mnemonic bar also has a representational significance thereby blending epistemic actions with manipulations of external representations.

Biological manipulations, epistemic actions and self-correcting actions are only three prongs of the cognitive integrationist's argument. The fourth is cognitive practices, the consideration of which must wait until Chapter 6. However, since representational manipulation occurs before we get even to the level of cognitive practices, we need a general account of the fundamental conditions for a representation. The conditions I provide (below) can cover both biological cases of representation, such as Millikan's intentional icons as well as diagrams, charts or other "conventional" representations. The conditions are supposed to reveal when something counts as a representation and under what circumstances it is repeatable, rather than a one off co-incidence or contrivance. The account gives us an understanding of representations both biological and cultural that form the core of the next two chapters.

4.4   Representation: The Peircean principle

The Peircean principle[8] maintains that any representation involves the following three components: a representational vehicle with representationally salient properties, an object or environmental property and a consumer that exploits the vehicle in virtue of its representationally salient properties.[9] The consumption of the vehicle in virtue of its salient properties helps to establish the vehicle's representational function, what it represents. The components together form a representational triad. The triad is repeatable only when certain conditions hold of the three components. I will go on to explain what these conditions are.

4.4.1 The three conditions for the repeatability of the representational triad

The first condition is that the vehicle has certain intrinsic or relational properties that make it salient to a consumer. The second condition is that the vehicle is exploited by a consumer in virtue of its salient properties, thereby establishing the vehicle's representational function (the function of representing an object/environmental property). The third condition is that a representational triad (a genuine representation) is established only when the representational function is recruited for some further end, such as the detecting of food. The recruitment of the representation in virtue of its function is established as a norm. Millikan (1984, 1993) shows how such norms are established as proper biological functions, but the norm might very well be conventional. The conditions can be unpacked in the following way.

4.4.2 The representational vehicle

A token vehicle Φ is a representational vehicle when it has properties that can *potentially* be exploited by a representational consumer.

A vehicle has properties either intrinsically or relationally, independently of its relation to a consumer. Potentially, these properties make it salient to a consumer, thereby establishing its function. For example, the vehicle can have intrinsic material properties that make it *iconic*. The most obvious sense in which a vehicle has iconic properties is that it shares some properties in common with an object. An image of a rose is red and the rose itself is red, the image is like the rose in this respect. But the mapping of properties may be more abstract, think of the mapping of the map of the London tube system onto the actual spatial layout of the tunnels and stations. An iconic vehicle has these properties independently of its relation to a consumer; but it is the vehicle's relation to a consumer that establishes the vehicle's function.

An *index* is a vehicle which stands in a dynamical or causal relation to its object – it has a relational property. Dark clouds are indexes of rain, rings in a tree are indexes of age, weathervanes are indexes of wind direction, barometers are indexes of atmospheric pressure. An *Index* is a vehicle, with a potential representational function, because it stands in a causal relation to an object/environmental property. It would not be an *index* if its object did not exist, but it will continue to stand in this relation whether or not it is exploited as a vehicle.

Vehicles have properties that make them salient to consumers. The properties are only potentially salient to a consumer. Until the representational function is established, they remain just properties of the vehicle. This point is expanded in the next section.

4.4.3 Representational salience

A token vehicle Φ is salient when it has properties that are potentially salient to a consumer. For example,

Φ is salient because it is causally correlated with an object/environmental property X, or with objects/environmental properties X, Y, Z. . . .

Therefore the properties a vehicle has intrinsically and/or relationally are *potentially* salient to a consumer. The function of the vehicle is not established just by the intrinsic properties of the vehicle itself, or by the vehicle's causal connection to its object. The former seems obvious, the caricature of Winston Churchill which Putnam's ant traces in the sand by its movements is only potentially a salient vehicle (Putnam 1981). In one sense it is just a trail left in the sand by an ant, but we can also consume it as a likeness of Churchill because of its iconic properties. The Peircean principle makes sense of why iconic vehicles get to have a representational function. The consumer makes the mapping of the icon onto its object, as opposed to the implausible claim that the icon maps itself.

Similarly, a vehicle that stands in a dyadic causal relation to its object does not represent by the mere fact of this relation. There is nothing in the brute causal relation itself which gives the vehicle its function. This is the case even if Φ is always caused by X. Say the motion of billiard ball B is always caused by billiard ball

A striking it, presumably no one thinks that because of this causal relation billiard ball B represents billiard ball A? But the case of the index, or the so-called "natural information," is no different.

For example, the 24 rings on a tree stump indicate that the tree is 24 years old (Dretske 1988, p. 55); however, trees do not develop growth rings to tell themselves or anyone else how old they are. Yet, the happy correlation of the number of growth rings with the age of the tree is potentially salient for a consumer.

This cannot be rebutted by the old line that if nothing indicates unless there is someone to whom it indicates, then one is committed to some form of implausible idealism (Dretske 1988, p. 55). Imagine that there is indeed a mechanism in trees that monitors the age of the tree and consumes the growth rings of the tree as an index of its age. This need not commit us to any implausible teleology, purposiveness or mindedness in nature – as Millikan has amply shown (1993).

The Peircean principle explains why the indexical vehicle is capable of becoming a representation, because it is exploited by a consumer – where the consumer need not be a mind or interpreter. So there is nothing in the intrinsic character (monadic) of a vehicle or the relation (dyadic) of a vehicle to its object that suffices to establish representational function. It is only when the properties of a vehicle are salient for a consumer that the vehicle has a representational function.

4.4.4   Representational function

Φ has a representational function when its salient features are exploited by some consumer Ψ. For example,

> Φ has the function of representing X for consumer Ψ, because Φ is causally correlated with an object/environmental property X.

The vehicle has properties independently of its relation to a consumer, but they are the very properties that are exploited by the consumer. Remember that a vehicle is salient for a consumer in some respect. Salience is determined by the relation a vehicle has to its object – iconic or indexical. For example, a weathervane represents the wind, not in all respects, but in respect of its direction. It is because the object stands in this relation to the vehicle, that it will be exploited in a particular way. This is how the function of Φ gets established.

4.4.5 The representational triad

The representational triad is established when the salient features of a vehicle are consumed towards some further end. The representational triad consists of a vehicle with salient properties that have a function because they are exploited by a consumer which recruits the vehicle to the production of some end, such as a particular behaviour.

The representational triad is thereby understood in terms of ends, these ends may be established by conscious intention in humans or by non-conscious and non-teleological biological functions. For this representational triad to be repeatable it must be established as a norm. For example,

Φ represents X for consumer Ψ for the biological function of detecting food.

Establishing a representational function requires the production and consumption of vehicles for some end. This process becomes repeatable when the normal conditions conspire to produce the representational triad, thereby making the representational process normative. These are the conditions under which representational triads are established. But now I must say something about the norms involved in making the triad repeatable.

According to Peirce there are three kinds of normative representational triads, following Liszka, we can call them *teleological, teleonomic* and *mechanical* (Liszka 1996, 33), although I shall say nothing about mechanical triads here. Teleonomic representational triads involve a biological proper function for the production and consumption of vehicles – see the next chapter for a full treatment (Millikan 1984, 1993). Teleological representational triads involve the production and consumption of vehicles according to the conventions of a symbolic system such as natural language.

It is important that teleonomic representational triads derive their normativity from purely natural processes; this gets normativity in the game from the outset.

Teleological representational triads involve conventional systems of vehicles, what Peirce calls symbols. Such a conventional symbolic system would be a natural language. Importantly, teleological representational triads are subject to growth and development, they are corrected over time by self-controlled actions, as opposed to natural selection.

So, take the growth and development of words in a natural language – or if you prefer concepts. The concept of water has developed from its being an element to its being H_2O. The word "cool" is used to refer to temperature in one context, it is used to refer to a disposition or character trait in another – "he's as cool as a cucumber", and something even more ineffable concerning fashion and popularity – "those trainers are cool." The production and consumption of teleological representational triads is flexible, context-dependent and open-ended and this differentiates it from the production and consumption of teleonomic representational triads.

The conditions for representation are simple: a vehicle is consumed in virtue of its salient properties, this makes sense of singular cases such as ant trails and clouds. However, for the repeatability of this representational triad we need the co-ordination of producer and consumer mechanisms, a vehicle is produced which is consumed for some further end. This process is established as a teleonomic norm if it is adaptively successful as in the case of Millikan's intentional icons.

The very same conditions for representation are the basis for teleological representational triads and repeatability requires the co-ordination of producer and consumer. However, the process is established as a teleological norm by being part of a conventional system such as language or mathematics. How we get from teleonomic norms to teleological norms need not detain us here (although I will discuss this at length in the next chapter).

The Peircean principle allows us to explain how representation works in both natural and social environments. It demonstrates the commonalities and differences between teleonomic and teleological representation and provides the very fundamental conditions under which representation is possible. It makes no commitment to whether representational triads are internal, external or distributed across body and world. I shall address this issue further in the next chapter.

4.5 Conclusion

We began this chapter with an account of our embodied engagements with the world and we saw how this was the basis for manipulating the environment. There are different, yet complementary, ways in which we manipulate the environment to complete cognitive tasks. These range from the biologically basic to the manipulation of external representations. How we have evolved these abilities is the topic of the next chapter.

5
The Evolution of the Hybrid Mind

> We are indeed part of nature, and are the products of mechanisms that made other species too. Nonetheless, we are very unusual primates indeed. This too must be acknowledged and explained.
>
> – Kim Sterelny

5.1 Introduction

In this chapter we shall look at the biological basis for cognitive integration. I aim to show that the manipulation thesis and the hybrid mind thesis both have a biological and evolutionary basis. This is because our biological understanding of organism–environment relations does not respect the standard boundaries between what is "internal" and "external" so often relied upon by philosophers and cognitive scientists. Such disrespect for boundaries is illustrated by the case of extended phenotypes. In general, organism–environment systems can be understood in terms of reciprocal coupling, with the organism and environmental niche mutually affecting one another.

The manipulation and hybrid mind theses have biological coupling at their base, as opposed to an asymmetric externalism where there is no significant level of feedback from organism to environment (Godfrey-Smith 1996). I shall also argue that biological reciprocal coupling is perfectly suited to adaptationist explanation.

I shall also show that biological cases of manipulation, epistemic actions and cognitive practices are all continuous with one another in evolutionary terms. This is because all three types of manipulation involve reciprocal coupling, but the most fundamental form of manipulation, biological coupling, sometimes involves manipulations of teleonomic representational triads of the kind described at the end of the last chapter. Millikan's account of teleonomic representation brings to the fore two important aspects of the biological basis of cognitive integration. First, it involves a kind of reciprocal coupling. Secondly, it involves biological normativity, in terms of adaptations, or Millikan's proper functions. This biological normativity is a pre-condition for the normativity of representation, often referred to as the possibility of misrepresentation. It follows that manipulations of external representations have an evolutionary basis – Mother Nature predisposes us to manipulate external representations.

The creation and manipulation of external representations is required to complete higher cognitive tasks, and cognitive practices are layered over the evolutionarily more basic biological coupling. Therefore, the hybrid mind exploits internal and external representations in the completion of cognitive tasks. This conclusion is also illustrated by the evolution of human cognition from hominids to *Homo sapiens*. Following Donald (1991) there are three stages of cognitive evolution: an episodic stage which is close to ape cognition, the oral–mythic stage where public language restructures and transforms our cognitive abilities and the theoretic stage where written systems of representation are created, stored and manipulated, giving rise to an abstract and theoretical form of cognition.

The argument of this chapter runs as follows:

1. Organisms are reciprocally coupled to their environmental niches. This is an organism–environment system as found in cases such as extended phenotypes.
2. As an organism–environment system the organism is predisposed to manipulate its environmental niche, or in some cases create it. This is an adaptation of the organism.
3. An organism's manipulations of its environment, whilst part of its phylogenetic history can, in many cases, be fine-tuned and calibrated through learning or reinforcement as part of its ontogenetic history.

4. That these manipulations are adaptations gives them a basic kind of normativity. This normativity allows for the beginnings of biological representations and there are many cases of organisms producing and consuming teleonomic representational triads.

5. Humans are predisposed to manipulate their environment, but the fine-tuning and calibration of these manipulations in ontogenesis is not part of their phylogenetic history. The role of culture in providing systems of teleological representational systems and methods for their manipulation must be learnt and practised before fluent bodily manipulations of external representations becomes part of the human's cognitive repertoire.

6. The phylogenetic history of *Homo sapiens* illustrates how we move on a continuum from biological manipulations as adaptations in our hominid forebears to more complicated forms of external representations and manipulations in tool use and imitation, through to language and the development of external representational systems. They all involve manipulations of the environment and eventually result in a culture which is a repository of representational systems that is passed on to later generations via learning and development.

5.2   Organism–environment systems

How should we understand the relation between an organism and its environment? Following Godfrey-Smith we might give an asymmetric externalist explanation of the relation between the organism and its environment; with its denial that there is any significant level of feedback from the organic system onto its environment (Godfrey-Smith 1996, p. 327).

By contrast we shall give an explanation of the relation in terms of what Dewey (1929) called organism–environment transactions and what I have been calling biological coupling. Dewey often denied the strict separation between mind and world in his epistemological work, but this denial came from a deeper source, from his views on organism–environment transactions. The transactions allow Dewey to bridge the gap between organism and environment because, although adaptations of organisms have evolved through the familiar process of natural selection (as neo-Darwinists understand it), it is not the case that a strong distinction between the organism and its environment need be made. Environment and organism do not go their own ways, they are often reciprocally coupled, as in the case of extended phenotypes.

Godfrey-Smith identifies a similarity between Dewey and Lewontin (1982, 1983) here, in that they both recognise a two-way interaction between organism and environment. Rather than the organism merely being the "passive" object of environmental selection pressures, the organism also reshapes its environment and alters... "the future course of the selection pressures to which they will have to respond" (Godfrey-Smith 1996, p. 327). As such, Dewey and Lewontin are advocating a biological version of the causal coupling identified in the second and the third chapters. The organism and its environment are reciprocally coupled, in the sense that the organism does not just passively reflect its environment, but through its responses and behaviours in turn affects that environment. This stands in contrast to the asymmetric understanding of both organism–environment transactions and adaptionist methodology.

We can see that the biologically coupled understanding of the adaptationist methodology is far more fruitful for the evolutionary biologist and, indeed, makes far more sense of biological phenomena such as extended phenotypes. I will argue for this by first looking at how biological coupling is already presupposed by biologists and philosophers of biology. The main point in favour of this claim is that the biologist already presupposes that the organism and environment are not strictly distinct and often form a "coupled system" in the sense of an extended phenotype (Dawkins 1982). Selective pressures upon the organism and environmental niche are built up by their reciprocal coupling, such that they co-evolve as a single system. In particular, we have the biological basis for the manipulation thesis and the hybrid mind thesis. This is because manipulations of the environment through reciprocal coupling are adaptations, and the organism–environment system is a hybrid system composed of both internal and external aspects.

The phylogenetic history of an organism establishes its manipulations of the environment as adaptations, but the ontogenetic history of the organism may include all sorts of fine-tuning of this adaptation, relative to niche, perhaps through learning history. This is specifically the case with humans who learn all sorts of ways in which their basic biological manipulations of the environment can be fine tuned to other purposes, which have not been selected for. This is where the importance of culture comes to the biological forefront. Furthermore, there are examples of the fine-tuning of manipulations in the niche construction of other species such as the Vogeltop bower birds of New Guinea (Avital and Jablonka 2000, Sterelny 2003).

We shall proceed by first looking at cases of extended phenotypes and organism–environment systems and then apply the adaptational methodology to them. Then we will look at how some criticisms of adaptationism seem to show that it is asymmetrically externalist; before finally demonstrating that the adaptationalist methodology is perfectly compatible with the biological coupling approach, I shall then turn to the questions of biological normativity, representation and the phylogenetic history of *Homo sapiens*.

5.2.1 Reciprocal coupling and extended phenotypes

Aspects of this approach are already familiar to biologists and philosophers of biology, in fact biologists often regard the distinction between organism and environment as fluid:

> For there is no clear line but only the most arbitrary demarcation between the organism considered as a process and its environment. The organismic process has no skin. It is constantly sucking in matter from its surroundings and spewing it out again. (Millikan 1993, 179)

Dawkins' treatment of the extended phenotype is a classic example of this attitude to the organism/environment distinction. The main point here being that the organism considered as a biological system extends out into the environment, often by incorporating or integrating with parts of the environment. There are many examples of the extended phenotype, here are just a few:

Birds build their nests out of materials found in their environments, twigs and so on, the snail builds its shell from calcium, gathered from ingested food, the Hermit crab, however, inherits the discarded shells of dead snails (Dawkins 1982). There would appear to be a commonsensical difference between these cases. The snail grows the shell as part of its body and we might think that it is equally part of its body as our skin or hair is. The hermit crab merely appropriates one for protection, and the bird constructs its nest out of things it finds around it rather than growing it as part of its body. Now take the case of caddis fly larvae, which walk around on riverbeds and construct their own "mobile homes" out of materials they find on the river bed.

> The house is a mobile home, carried about as the caddis walks, like the shell of a snail or hermit crab except that the animal builds it instead of growing it or finding it. Some species of caddis use sticks as building materials, others fragments of dead leaves, others small snail shells. But perhaps the most impressive caddis houses are the ones built in local stone. The caddis chooses its stones carefully, rejecting those that are too large or too small for the current gap in the wall, even rotating each stone until it achieves the snuggest fit. (Dawkins 1976, p. 238)

The caddis fly incorporates elements of all the three cases above: it secretes a cementing substance to bind the materials, it uses parts of its environment to construct the home and it appropriates shells discarded by other animals. What is the relevant difference between the caddis fly larvae and its "mobile home" and the snail and its "home grown" shell? The commonsensical difference would appear to be irrelevant here, for the purposes of biological explanation. The relevant difference cannot be that to be a part of an organism that part must be grown by the organism. The nest of the bird, the shell of the hermit crab and the home of the caddis fly are all as essential to the survival of these organisms as the shell of the snail.[1] In a stronger sense, these features are adaptations, or as Millikan calls them, "proper biological functions." They are part of the biological apparatus of the organism and subject to the same selective pressures, as we would consider other parts of the organism to be under. Millikan makes the same point in terms of what is spatially "inside" the system and what is spatially "outside."

> The bird needs its nest to function properly in exactly the same way that it needs, on the other hand, its skin and feathers and, on the other, its seeds. The nest, the feathers, and the seeds [food] are all part of the same organismic system. Conversely, the immune systems of the bird are designed to deal precisely with things

spatially inside its body but that are not part of the biological system. The distinction between what is spatially "inside" and what is spatially "outside" the bird, as such, has no significance for the study of the avian biological *system*. The only interesting principled distinction that can be drawn between that portion of the organismic system that is the organism proper and that portion of it that is normal environment is not determined by a spatial boundary. (Millikan 1993, p. 159)

What is and is not considered to be part of the organismic system is dependent upon a notion of adaptation and natural selection. Evolution allows the organismic system to be hybrid.

In the next section, I will begin to explain how extended phenotypes are explained in terms of adaptation. Before doing so, I will just mention that the very notion of adaptation I am about to refer to, which vindicates the notion of the extended phenotype and the rejection of a strict distinction between organism and environment, has been seen as the very vindicator of such a strict distinction! In other words, it is a form of asymmetric externalism, as defined in Chapter 2. Clearly, there are some issues to be resolved here.

5.3 Extended phenotypes and adaptation

Evolution occurs through the continuing process of adaptation. As a process, adaptation confers advantage upon organisms which are organised in such a way that their parts have functions which allow them to better *survive* in their environment. Adaptation is also used when talking about the "purpose" (biological) of the function of some structure, more will be said about this later.

Organisms are adapted to an ecological position, called a niche, rather than the entire environment.[2] There are general adaptations which may be shared by species in a group of related organisms – flying birds all have wings, feathers, beaks and so on. There are also special adaptations which some species have and others lack; for example, we can specify four adaptations of the woodpecker for the function of digging out insect grubs from the bark of trees, in its ecological niche. (1). The woodpecker has two toes on each foot, which are turned backwards such that the animal can get better purchase on the bark. (2). The tail feathers stiffen and serve to balance the animal as it bores into the bark. (3). The woodpecker bores a hole into the bark with a strong beak. (4). The woodpecker has an exceptionally long tongue, which it uses to remove the insect larvae at the bottom of the hole, for ingestion. Of course, there will be variants on these adaptations within woodpecker species depending upon the differences in their niches, for example different types of trees.

These adaptations do not happen by magic or by purposive design. Adaptations are the result of natural selection. We can understand natural selection quite simply. Within a population of organisms, individuals are not identical, rather there is variation in structure and function. This variation occurs randomly; however, some variations allow their possessors to function more efficiently in their ecological niche, competing better for food for example, than those who do not possess the variation. As such, they are better adapted to their niches, even if the variation only consists in a minute difference. The assumption is that these organisms which are better adapted to their niches will live longer, reproduce more abundantly and leave more of their progeny to reproduce, and they will exhibit greater *fitness*. Variations in a population will result in differences in fitness and

> natural selection results in the differential reproduction of those individuals whose variations (read "structural and functional capabilities"- their phenotype) provide them and their progeny with statistical advantages in adapting to environmental change or in competing with individuals of the same or different species. (Edelman 1992, p. 42)

Obviously these variations can only persist through generations if they are passed, during reproduction, from parents to offspring. In other words, adaptive traits (variations) are inherited by offspring which, because they have increased fitness, are more likely to proliferate the adaptive trait throughout the species. The variations are passed on from parent to offspring by discrete hereditary particles – genes. The actual unit of variation is the gene. This is because the gene is the unit of inheritance; genes determine the inheritance of a particular characteristic or group of characteristics. As such, only variations in genes can be inherited by offspring (Dawkins 1976).

Variations in genes are called mutations and arise randomly. Their persistent presence in the gene pool is not random, but the effect of natural selection. The genes inherited by an offspring constitute its genotype, which influences the development of the offspring from embryo to adulthood. Phenotypes – entire organisms, including organs, functions and behaviours – are the effects of genes.

Natural selection effects genes, but it cannot do so directly since genes are not presented to the environment, rather they do so through phenotypes. Traits of phenotypes such as – tails, shells, muscles and functions, the ability to run fast, to see more clearly, to be better camouflaged – are directly presented to natural selection. Differences in genes produce different phenotypic effects – genes are selected for in that they give rise to phenotypes which have selective advantages over their competitors. Phenotypes that are better at surviving and reproducing will contribute more genes to the gene pool, hence the phenotypic effects of those genes will occur in successive generations. In a nutshell, adaptations are phenotypical effects of genes that have been selected for and promote the replication of those genes which gave rise to those very phenotypes (Dawkins 1976).

Returning to the environment/organism distinction, it is clear that the phenotypical effects of genes extend beyond the body of the organism housing the gene, incorporating aspects of the environmental niche into the organismic system as extended phenotypes. These extended phenotypical effects of genes are adaptations in the sense just defined above, and so the adaptationist methodology is not asymmetrically externalist.

Extended phenotypical effects show that the organism/environment distinction can be fluid. The concept of biological coupling has some important explanatory work to do when considering the organism–environment system. This is why the adaptational approach to the organism–environment system is so important. The wide capacities and embodied manipulations of previous chapters can be understood in terms of biological adaptations.

In the next section, I will show how the organism–environment system as biologically coupled is quite consistent with the adaptational approach.

5.3.1 Biological coupling and adaptation

The adaptational approach I have been endorsing has come under heavy fire in recent times.[3] The main criticism of it is that it is a flawed methodology. I will proceed by saying a little more about the adaptationist methodology. I will then list the criticisms of it and defend the indispensability of the methodology to evolutionary biology. Finally, and most importantly, I will show how the adaptationist methodology is perfectly compatible with biological coupling.

The adaptationist methodology begins with "why" questions, for example, why is it that vultures have wings with a wide surface area and slotted edges and albatrosses have wings with a narrow surface area and smooth edges? Because vultures' wings are adapted to the aerodynamics required for soaring flight and albatrosses' wings are adapted to the aerodynamics of sailing flight. Soaring flight requires upcurrents of air and sailing flight requires horizontal air movement. The two species are differently adapted to the differing atmospheric conditions of their environmental niches.

Why do penguins still have wings if they do not fly? Because they use their wings when "flying" underwater, the biological function of their wings is adapted to movement through their ecological niche, the sea, at least in terms of their hunting environment. The adaptational methodology gives an answer to the "why" question in terms of the function of a structure such as a wing. Merely staring at the structure will not give us an answer to the "why" question. Only in considering what function the structure might have relative to its environmental niche, and given the constraints of natural selection and genotypical variation discussed above, can we have a reasonable answer to the question.

This is not uncontroversial. The adaptationist programme has been dubbed the "Panglossian paradigm" by the evolutionary biologist S.J. Gould. This is because adaptation is supposed to entail optimality of fitness. Lewontin takes the adaptational methodology to assume without proof that all aspects of the morphology, physiology and behaviour of organisms are adaptive optimal solutions to problems (Lewontin 1979).

The criticisms of the adaptational methodology, that we will consider, centre on four main points:

1. Gould and Lewontin (1979) point out that adaptational explanations are unfalsifiable. This is partly because of the supposed generality of such explanations, but also the actual methodology involved – which Gould and Lewontin liken to story

telling: "Since the range of adaptive stories is as wide as our minds are fertile, new stories can always be postulated. And if a story is not immediately available, one can always plead temporary ignorance and trust that it will be forthcoming" (Gould and Lewontin 1979, p. 153).

2. The first criticism is tightly connected to the second – the adaptational methodology is panglossian in that adaptations are always optimal, evolution is an optimising process.

3. Hereditary variation can be achieved by mechanisms other than natural selection. Not all phenotypic effects are adaptations. Some are due to neutral factors such as genetic drift, pleiotropy and allemotry.

4. Adaptations are defined in terms of how an organism becomes adapted to its environment. How does the traditional neo-Darwinist view of adaptation incorporate the reciprocal coupling at the centre of cognitive integration?

Let us begin with points 1 and 2. Not all improvements are adaptations (see point 3), so how can we tell if a function has been selected for, if it is an adaptation? The adaptive methodology is not algorithmic, but all adaptationists should take other possible factors into account when trying to decide whether an organ/function is an adaptation. For example, flying fish leap from the water, this should be explained adaptively, that they fall back into the water should not. The latter is merely a matter of physics, so where a physical explanation suffices adaptation is irrelevant.[4]

Some adaptations give rise to further functions that are not selected for: the woodpecker's beak has been adapted to boring into bark in search of insect larvae. The beak may also be useful for grooming, but it has not been adapted to perform this function – it is a happy by-product of the adapted function.

In considering whether an organ/function is an adaptation, we must pay close attention to the ecological niche of the organism, this is especially important when attempting to reconstruct exactly what the "purpose" of the organ/function is. The imaginative flights of fancy alluded to by Gould and Lewontin must be constrained by environmental factors. This is well illustrated by the case of the sponge. Sponges feed by filtering water through themselves. This filtering process is achieved by flagella which pump water through the sponge. However, whilst the flagella have been adapted for the purpose of pumping, to achieve feeding, this is not the full story of the adaptation. The sponge also uses the water currents of its surroundings to aid its pumping. Vogel describes the process:

> The structure of sponges is most exquisitely adapted to take advantage of such currents, with clear functions attaching to a number of previously functionless features. Dynamic pressure on the incurrent openings facing upstream, valves closing incurrent pores lateral and downstream, and suction from the large distal or apical excurrent openings combine to gain advantage from even relatively slow currents. And numerous observations suggest that sponges usually prefer moving water. Why did so much time elapse before someone made a crude model of a sponge, placed it in a current and watched a stream of dye pass through it? (Vogel 1981, p. 190)

The pumping adaptation of the sponge cannot be properly described unless we take into account its immediate surroundings, its environmental niche (Clark 1989). This involves not just recognising what kind of environment the organism is situated in – water, air and so on – but looking at how the organism might exploit various features of its immediate surroundings to perform a particular function – the pumping of the sponge's flagella. This involves approaching adaptations in a particular way: specifically the biologist should not look only at the narrow features of the organism, but look at how the adaptive function is properly related to its environment. In Millikan's terms, we are describing how the adaptive function fits into the organism–environment system. This is the same as saying that the sponge is reciprocally coupled to its environment – they are mutually constraining.

This leads us directly to the second point. The adaptational approach is not panglossian because it assumes that evolution is an optimising process. To understand why this is the case we must ask the question, "optimal relative to what?" The optimising process may actually be a satisficing process, where the adaptation would be a locally optimal state rather than a globally optimal state.

Natural selection may be a satisficing process, in other words, an adaptation may be a satisfactory "solution" to a "problem" reaching a locally optimal state. The pumping adaptation of the sponge is an example of a locally optimal solution to the problem of feeding in its environmental niche. However, this may not be the best possible solution in "global" terms, for example a design could be invented by a creator, such as ourselves, which would be far more elegant, cost effective and so on. However, in terms of available physiological structure and environmental niche, as well as "cost" issues, the sponge's solution may be the "locally" optimal solution. If satisficing is sufficient for the constraints of survival and reproduction, then there is no reason why natural selection should be "optimising" in any stronger sense.

An analogy with error-minimising (hence optimising as satisficing) learning techniques, as discussed in Churchland and Sejnowski, 1992, Chapter 3, is instructive here. Development and learning in nervous systems is describable by a cost function:

> This is just to state the familiar thesis of natural selection in a neurobiological context: the modifications to nervous systems that are preserved are by and large those modifications that contribute to (at least do not undermine) the organism's survival in its niche. . . . in other words, by dint of parameter adjusting procedures, (such as back-propagation and competitive learning) nervous systems, ontogenetically and phylogenetically, appear to be finding local minima in their error surfaces. (Churchland and Sejnowski 1992, p. 133–5)

Nervous systems have been modified according to selective forces, these forces appear to be error minimising, analogous to error-minimising techniques in artificial neural networks. However, in descending the error gradient the nervous systems that are selected for should not be considered as the best of all possible nervous systems. This is because error minimisation is only a satisficing process – in the sense that, given in place structure and environmental niche, the process will find a "satisfactory" local minimum.

Gradient descent learning algorithms in neural networks, such as back-propagation, allow the network to find a point in weight space which is a good solution – a local minimum. There are, however, many such minima within a weight space, and a network which begins with randomly set weights is not forced into finding only one of the minima, but must blindly search through the weight space until it finds one of them.

This is a nice analogy for natural selection as a satisficing process, the finishing position may only be a local minimum, there are many possible local minima, and natural selection is not necessarily forced down any particular one of them. Natural selection can be thought of as satisficing, rather than optimising, but just how are we conceiving of "optimal" and "optimising" here? This is why we must ask "optimal relative to what?"

The answer is relative to in place constraints such as existing physiology and environmental niche. An optimal adaptation for birds would seem to be the development of propellers, so if natural selection is an optimising process, why have not birds developed propellers? Because "you can't grow a vertebrate with propellers" (Pinker 1997, p. 169). The developmental constraints on birds preclude this possible adaptation.

Taking a more serious example, the structure of the albatross's wing (narrow surface area with smooth edges) is an adaptation relative to the developmental constraints of the organism and its ecological niche. Whilst the adaptation may have been produced by the "satisficing" procedure of natural selection, reaching a local minimum, this may be locally optimal as opposed to globally optimal. From the vantage point of global optimality the albatross's adaptation may appear far from optimal, an optimising designer might be able to develop wings which are superior aeronautically to the albatross's and we might conclude that adaptations are not optimal solutions.

Therefore, natural selection as an optimising process does not entail maximally optimal solutions – solutions that ignore relevant constraints – as the birds growing propellers example shows. The criticism of adaptationism by natural selection as an optimising solution is based upon this mistaken assumption. Take the following example, inspired by Dennett (1987, p. 264).

Imagine a bunch of shipwrecked sailors, who decide to construct a sailboat from local materials. We shall assume that the sailors are not experts in the design of sailing ships; in fact they are ignorant of the niceties of the aerodynamics which inform the construction of sails and masts. The resulting sailboat may look inferior to the expertly designed sailboat from which they were originally marooned, but relative to their conditions, available materials and tools, it is the optimal design.

The applicability of optimality of design is only relevant within the given constraints. Applying a notion of optimality which ignores these constraints, a sailboat constructed by experts with prime materials, is not only unfair but a misunderstanding of the use of the term "optimal" in these cases. Optimising, considered as reaching a local minimum, does not support the panglossian paradigm of Gould and Lewontin. Furthermore, there is nothing in this account of optimisation that conflicts with the notion of reciprocal coupling, or extended phenotypes. We can see that the caddis fly larvae's adaptation to its niche (the riverbed) is a local minimum given the environmental and physical constraints. The locally optimal solution found through natural selection does not respect the commonsensical boundary between organism and environment, it allows for them to be reciprocally coupled.

This should put the worries of points 1 and 2 to rest. Point 3 should not worry us unduly, since it is unlikely that genetic drift is responsible for adaptations such as that of the caddis fly larvae. We have also resolved the alleged incompatibility of the coupling of organism and environment with an adaptationist methodology, thereby dealing with point 4. We have seen that reciprocal coupling can be explained in terms of adaptation to an environmental niche through natural selection.

Having established that organism-environment systems that are reciprocally coupled and involve the organism manipulating its environment are adaptations, I now want to look at some examples of the fine-tuning of these manipulative adaptations through mechanisms of inheritance that are not themselves adaptive.

The Vogeltop bowerbird presents a fascinating example of "cultural" fine-tuning of a manipulative adaptation. The male bowerbird builds a structure which is used to entice the female bowerbird into mating. However, Vogeltops living in one area of New Guinea build quite different bowers to those constructed by Vogeltops living in a different area (Sterelny 2003, p. 151). The birds living on the Kumawa mountains build towers of sticks surrounded by a mat constructed of dead moss fibres, as Sterelny puts it, "painted" with its own excrement and decorated with leaves and acorns (Sterelny 2003, p. 151). The Vogeltops living on the Wandamen mountains construct a bower which is more like a hut, with a surround of live green moss decorated very brightly and no painting with excrement involved.

Sterelney conjectures, following Avital and Jablonka (2000), that this change within species does not appear to be a genetic change, but a cultural one. Genetically, both Kumawan and Wandamen Vogeltops are predisposed to construct bowers, but this manipulative capacity has found different expressions in the two populations.

Similarly New Caledonian crows appear to be able to fine-tune their tool construction according to what is available to them (Hunt 1996, Weir *et al.* 2002, Sterelny 2003). In the wild, the crow fashions its own tools from twigs and leaves. The twig involves a hook at one end for probing and the removal of extraneous leaves and bark from the other end for gripping. The crow carries the tool with it for continued use rather than just discarding it after successfully prising prey from its hiding place. This ability is remarkable enough on its own, but Weir *et al.* report that a captive crow was able to take a piece of wire and bend it into an appropriate shape for accessing otherwise inaccessible food.

Therefore, the fine-tuning of manipulative abilities is something found across species. It will come as no surprise that the human species is expert at niche construction and manipulation and that these abilities are fine-tuned by cultural inheritance and accumulation of change. I shall return to this issue in Section 5.5.1.

I turn now to filling in some of the details required for the biological basis of cognitive integration. Millikan's biosemantics incorporates both reciprocal coupling and a biological normativity derived from adaptation. I shall apply Millikan's account of teleonomic representation to several examples. This will lead us immediately to the issue of the relation between biological coupling and cognitive coupling.

5.4   Biological normativity and representation

Millikan uses a well-established notion of biological function and highlights the normativity of biological functions. Millikan's understanding of proper biological functions allows us to understand how there could be teleonomic representation in the biological world. As we saw in the previous chapter, teleonomic representation involves the production and consumption of representational vehicles for some end. Millikan shows that the production and consumption of representational vehicles, what she calls intentional icons, are biological functions, and the normativity of teleonomic representations is derived from the normativity of biological functions. What is important for us is that the examples of teleonomic representation involve reciprocally coupled processes and that these are biological functions (adaptations).

5.4.1　Proper functions

Millikan's original definition of a proper function is as follows:

> A function F is a direct proper function of x if x exists having a character C, because by having C it can perform F. (Millikan 1984, p. 26)

The definition is historical because x's being able to perform F is dependent upon C and is made possible "because there were things that performed F in the past due to having C" (Millikan 1984, p. 26).

Proper functions are normative, in the sense that a device might have a proper function even though it fails to perform it. Here the possibility of misrepresentation might be made clear. Millikan's example is as follows:

> It is the biological purpose of the sperm to swim until it reaches an ovum. That is what its tail is for. But very few sperm actually achieve this biological end because ova are in such short supply. (Millikan 1993, p. 223)

What allows for the continuance of a proper function throughout generations? For a device/organism to have a proper function, it must share this function in common with its ancestors. You and I both have hearts which pump blood, because we share a common ancestor whose heart had the proper function of pumping blood. Proper functions are copied and reproduced through generations. However, we know (according to the best neo-Darwinian accounts) that no heart is directly copied from any other heart, rather, it is genes which are directly copied and it is these genes which have the proper function of producing hearts.[5] Karen Neander has a snappy definition of this:

Def: Some effect (Z) is the proper function of some trait (X) in organism (O) iff the genotype responsible for X was selected for doing Z, because doing Z was adaptive for O's ancestors. (Neander 1995, p. 111)

Proper functions are to be understood in terms of the normal conditions under which the device performs the proper function; and normal explanations which explain... "the performance of a particular function, telling how it was (typically) historically performed on those (perhaps rare) occasions when it was properly performed" (Millikan 1993, p. 86). In understanding what a device's proper function is, we appeal to normal conditions; these norms are understood in terms of natural selection and selection is a historical process.

5.4.2 Example: Bee dances

The normal explanation of the performance of a proper function makes reference to the normal conditions under which, historically, the proper function has been performed and selected for. This can be seen in the bee dance example (see diagram below, based upon Hutto 1999):

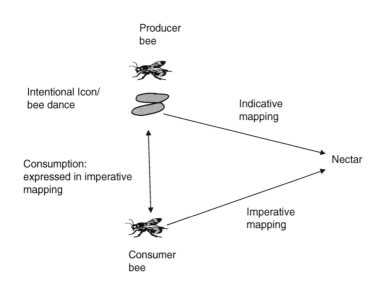

Producer bee

Intentional Icon/ bee dance

Indicative mapping

Consumption: expressed in imperative mapping

Nectar

Imperative mapping

Consumer bee

There are mechanisms in bees which have the proper function of producing a bee dance. There are also mechanisms in bees which have the proper function of consuming bee dances. The proper function of the bee dance producer (more strictly the relational proper function, because the function is related to something in the organism's environment) is to produce the consequence that consumer bees fly off in the direction of the orientation of the bee dance. The relational proper function of the bee dance producer is selected for iff in normal conditions it has, historically, led bees to find flowers, pollen, nectar, food – that which optimises survival value. The consumer mechanism gets selected for iff, under normal conditions it has, historically, produced behaviour leading to flowers, nectar and so on; on the basis of the consumed bee dances.

The producer and consumer bees are reciprocally coupled to one another. The producer mechanism has the function of producing intentional icons *for* consumer mechanisms and consumer mechanisms have the function of consuming the intentional icons produced by producer mechanisms for some further end. This requires that the producer and the consumer mechanisms can only function properly if they are both present and coordinating; this is the normal condition for the mechanisms to function properly.

The producer and the consumer bees are also reciprocally coupled to the environment. A normal condition of the environment, the location of nectar, has the effect of producing bee dances. These have the effect of sending consumer bees to the location of the nectar. This in turn produces two normal conditions in the environment, the nectar being located in the hive and flowers being pollinated at the first location of the nectar.

For the mechanisms to function properly the normal conditions must be in place. It is quite easy to see how contingent factors could interfere with the normal conditions of proper functioning, but this is why biological functions are normative; it is the proper function of mechanisms in normal conditions that is selected for. The next issue concerns why the bee dance is a teleonomic representation.

5.4.3   Teleonomic representation

Is this really representation? First the distinction between proper functioning and malfunctioning looks secure. This could, in principle, underwrite the normative notion of content demanded by the possibility of misrepresentation. Secondly, the relationality of some proper functions gives them an intentional aspect, in Brentano's sense, they are directed at something beyond themselves. The intentional icons have three properties:

1 They are relationally adapted to some feature of the world.
2 The relation can be seen in terms of a "mapping."
3 The icons have the proper function of guiding a consumer mechanism in performing its proper function.

If the relational conditions for this bee dance (qua intentional icon) are normal, then it will successfully map the location of flowers and so on. (indicative mapping). If this is successful, then the icon directs the consumer bee to the location of nectar (imperative mapping). It is in the consumption of an icon that the representational function is established. The direct proper function of an icon is the effect it ought to produce (sending consumer bees in the direction of nectar), not what it statistically does produce.

> Intentional icons do not, as such or in general, carry "natural information." Nor do they "covary" with or "track" what they icon. Their definition makes no reference to how likely or unlikely they are actually to correspond to their designated environmental features, nor how likely these features are to get mapped by them. (Millikan 1993, p. 107)

Millikan provides an account of biological norms and how representation can arise according to these norms. Her account of teleonomic representations falls under the Peircean Principle as outlined in Chapter 4. In the next section, I will apply Millikan's account of biological representation to a case of reciprocal coupling that has already been explored by cognitive integrationists.

5.4.4 Biosemantics and reciprocal coupling

The example of reciprocal coupling we shall now turn to is cricket phonotaxis (Clark 2001a). Barbara Webb explains the process of phonotaxis in crickets as a kind of coupled process. "Phonotaxis is the process whereby a female cricket identifies a male of the same species by his song, turns in his direction, and reliably locomotes to the source" (Clark 2001a, p. 127). This process does not entail, according to Webb, a detailed internal representation of the male song, or an internal representation of the environment by which the female cricket plots her course. The explanation of this process is based upon Wheeler and Clark (1999).

The female cricket has two ears, one on each foreleg. The ears are connected to one another by a tracheal tube; this tube is also connected to openings on the body called "spiracles." The male cricket's song arrives to the female cricket either directly to the ear nearest the sound source or via the other ear, spiracles and tracheal tube. This makes a difference, because the two routes take different amounts of time to reach the eardrum on the side nearest to the male cricket's song. This has the effect of making the

> amplitude of ear-drum vibration . . . higher on the side nearer the source. In short there is a direction-dependent intensity difference at the female's ears, with the side closer to the sound source having the stronger response. (Wheeler and Clark 1999, p. 105)

The cricket is able to locomote in the direction of the song in virtue of an interneurone which is connected to the ear, which when activated by the stronger vibration turns the cricket in its direction. This is an extra important feature of the activity of these interneurones, summarised by Wheeler and Clark as,

> Each of the two dedicated interneurones in the female's nervous system has a decay time during which, after firing, it gradually returns to its non-activated rest state. During this recovery period, a neurone is nearer to its firing threshold than if it were at rest. In consequence, if a neurone receives input during the decay time, it will fire again more quickly than if it receives input during the decay time, it will fire again more quickly than if it receives that input while at rest. So, if the gaps between the syllables of the male's song were shorter than the total decay time it will fire again more quickly than if it receives that input while at rest. (Wheeler and Clark 1999, p. 106)

This is important, because if, for example, the male cricket's song was continuous, it would be difficult to tell which of the interneurons had fired first, since the interneurones reach their threshold at the beginning of the cricket's song. Thus the temporal and acoustic pattern of the cricket's song is important. The syllables and gaps between them in the male cricket's song must be synchronised with the activation threshold of the female cricket's interneurones. Wheeler and Clark claim that this shows that "... the temporal pattern of male's song is constrained by the activation profile of the dedicated interneurones in the female" (Wheeler and Clark 1999, p. 106).

We could also say that the activation profile of the dedicated interneurones is constrained by the temporal pattern of the male's song. But, if this is supposed to be a coupled process, that is a reciprocal one, it would be better to claim that the temporal pattern and interneurone activation profile are mutually constraining. Otherwise it looks as if we have an asymmetrically externalist explanation, and the reciprocal nature of the coupling of the male song and interneurones will be lost.

In Millikan's terms, the producer mechanism has the proper function of producing the song for the consumer mechanism, the female's interneurones. Just as in the bee dance case, the producer and the consumer mechanisms can only function properly if they are both present and coordinating – this is the normal condition for the mechanisms to function properly.

So far, so good. However, Webb considers her explanation of phonotaxis in crickets and robotic crickets not to involve any "inner representations," nor any classical style explanations. This might make us think that explaining phonotaxis in Millikanian terms is inappropriate because it involves representations. Indeed Webb denies that a representational interpretation of the activation profile of the interneurones is useful.

> It is not necessary to use this symbolic interpretation to explain how the system functions: the variables serve a mechanical function in connecting sensors to motors, a role epistemologically comparable to the function of the gears connecting the motors to the wheels [of a car]. (Webb 1994, p. 53)

Clark (2001a) concurs with Webb's characterisation of the robot/ cricket functions:

> Understanding the behaviour of the robot cricket requires atten-
> tion to features that, from the standpoint of classical cognitive
> science, look more like details of implementation (the fixed length
> of the trachea, the syllable repetition rate of the male) than
> substantive features of an intelligent control system. (Clark 2001a,
> p. 128)

However, the beauty of Millikan's account of teleonomic representations is that it does not involve classical representations with
constituent structure. It is for this reason that the concern of Webb
and Clark to keep the description only at the mechanical level is ill
founded.

Cognitive integrationists are right to highlight that these and many
other examples of biological coupling demonstrate the importance
of the interactive coupling between an organism and features of its
environment. Once we recognise this "causal spread", we must give
the environmental features their due explanatory role. This requires
that we develop the kind of explanation that will be sensitive to
the interactive coupling between the organism and its environment.
An explanation which places too heavy a burden upon the internal
structure of the organism will not be sensitive to the causal interactions between the organism and its environment. This is why Webb
(1994), Brooks (1991), Thelen and Smith (1994) and others have
rejected the traditional explanatory methods that rely upon "internal
representations" and models of the world.

However, a merely causal explanation of the coupled process is
insufficient. We need to provide a biologically normative account
of phonotaxis. This is because a merely causal account does not
tell us why the cricket's song and interneurones are reciprocally
coupled. It certainly tells us how they are reciprocally coupled, but
an adaptationist explanation will also tell us why. As such, we want
to think of biological cases of coupling, not just in terms of being
a causal relation, but also in terms of being biologically normative.
Millikan's account of biological normativity and teleonomic representation allows us to understand why the cricket song and interneurones function as they do.

To summarise, the production of intentional icons is normative in
that it is dependent upon the history of the mechanism that produces
them. Intentional icons can have both indicative and imperative

effects on consumer mechanisms, the relations of interest loop out into the world, and the icons do not have to be symbols internal to the organisms in question. The normative function of the icon is in place only when the relations between it, the object(s) it maps onto and the consumer mechanism are in place together as an irreducible triad (the Peircean principle). Because of this we can see that the normative structure of Millikan's account can be mapped onto coupled biological processes, such as cricket phonotaxis.

However, the relation between producer and consumer mechanisms *could* be entirely located within the skin of an organism. Millikan makes this clear: "Put (an analogue of) the bee dance inside the body so that it mediates between two parts of the same organism and you have . . . an inner representation" (1993, p. 164). The beauty of the Peircean principle is that it is entirely agnostic as to the location of the representational triad.

As such, it is unimportant whether or not the relation between producer and consumer mechanism is spatially inside or spatially outside the organism. Although Webb denies the need for any internal representations, it is possible to see the male cricket as a producer mechanism which produces an intentional icon that has an indicative and imperative effect over the female cricket as a consumer mechanism. The male and female crickets are causally coupled, but they are also normatively coupled as well. The objection against a classical analysis is that there are no symbolic representations present in the phonotaxis case. Granted, Millikan's account of teleonomic representation does not involve classical representations. The consumer of the intentional icon acts on the basis of an imperative, not as a conceptual interpretation of the icon. Manipulations of external representations have an evolutionary basis – Mother Nature predisposes us to manipulate external representations.

The question we must now address is whether the explanatory model given to us by the examples of biological coupling applies to cases of cognitive coupling and whether the explanatory moral follows.

5.5 Biological coupling as cognitive coupling

So far, I have given the evolutionary conditions under which there is continuity between biological coupling and cognitive coupling.

We should think of this in the following way: in the biological cases, external vehicles and manipulations of those vehicles are extended phenotypical effects. This should be taken in the general sense that natural selection does not respect the discrete organism. The organism's adaptation to its niche involves no strict separation between organism and niche; as the examples of extended phenotypes show, the organism and its niche can co-evolve as a single system through reciprocal coupling. This gives us a plausible basis for thinking that the evolution of cognition will similarly involve reciprocal coupling – hence the evolution of capacities to manipulate external vehicles.

In this section, I return to the manipulation thesis. To begin with I will look at an example of cognitive coupling closest to biological coupling and then move on to manipulations of external representations.

We have already scouted perception as being a case of biological coupling in the previous chapter, through the sensorimotor approach.

Churchland, Ramachandran and Sejnowski (1994) and Ballard (1991) claim that it may appear as if we have a rich inner representation of the current visual scene, but actually there is no constant stable inner representation, rather we perform fast saccades, retrieving information as and when required (Clark 1999). Clark identifies the major claims of interactive and animate theories of perception as follows (Clark 1999, p. 8):

1. Daily agent–environment interactions often do not require the construction and use of detailed inner models of the full visual scene.
2. Low-level perception may "call" motor routines that yield better perceptual input and hence improve information pick-up.
3. Real-world actions may sometimes play an important role in the computational process itself.
4. The internal representation of worldly events and structures may be less like a passive data-structure or description and more like a direct recipe for action.

Yarbus (1967), Ballard (1991) and Churchland, Ramachandran and Sejnowski (1994) found that perception is dependent upon scanning by saccadic eye movements and that scanning by saccades is highly task-directed.

> Evidence for proposition 1 comes from a series of experiments in which subjects watch images on a computer screen. Subjects are allowed to examine an on-screen pictorial display. Then, as they continue to saccade around the scene (focusing first on one area, then another) small changes are made to the currently unattended parts of the display. The changes are made during the visual saccades. It is an amazing fact that, for the most part, quite large changes go unnoticed: changes such as the replacement of a tree by a shrub, or the addition of a car, deletion of a hat and so on. Why do such gross alterations remain undetected? A compelling hypothesis is that the visual system is not even attempting to build a rich, detailed model of the current scene but is instead geared to using frequent saccades to retrieve information as and when it is needed for some specific problem-solving purpose. This fits nicely with Yarbus' classic (Yarbus, 1967) finding that the pattern of such saccades varies (even with identical scenes) according to the type of task the subject has been set (e.g. to give the ages of the people in a picture, to guess the activity they have been engaged in, etc.). (Clark 1999, p. 9)

We do not build stable, complex internal representations of the environment via perception, instead we scan for what we need because the environment provides the constant variables. Hence, we do not notice changes to parts of the scene that we have already saccaded over, because we rely upon the environment to remain constant, rather than internally scanning a stable representation of the environment. Thus, there is a continuous interactive loop between the local visual environment and the visual mechanisms.

This is an example of cognition that involves manipulations of the environment through biological coupling. The adaptation of the visual system to the environmental niche of the organism is much like the adaptation of the sponge to its niche, because the visual system is directly coupled to the environment. So biological coupling can be a class of cognitive coupling. However, can we identify a continuity between biological coupling and other forms of cognitive manipulations such as cognitive practices?

Certain specific tasks are possible because we have developed symbolic representational schemes, arithmetical, geometrical and logical for example, which allow us to perform certain kinds of cognitions. These cognitions depend upon our ability to manipulate these representations. Here we are in the realm of cognitive practices.

Cognitive practices allow us to do things that we cannot do in our heads such as solving mathematical problems, composing papers, using a sketch pad. We learn how to use representational systems and the tools and media in which they are embodied. This process of learning and development transforms our cognitive capacities. For example, the capacity for linguistic systematicity is gained through the process of language learning. We gain the capacity for mathematical cognition through gaining mastery over mathematics (see Chapters 6 and 7 for further discussion). Being coupled to external representations and tools is a fundamental aspect of this transformative process. However, we will have only a partial understanding of what is going on by focusing on the coupling relation alone.

A merely causal account, in terms of causal coupling, of how this happens will not explain *why* manipulations of the external artefact is part of cognition; it will merely provide evidence that it is. Remember that the causal coupling between the interneurones of the female cricket and the acoustic patterns of the cricket's song demonstrate that there is an important interaction between the organism and its environment. That there are a series of pattern recognition and completion routines coupled with the iterated updating of numerals on a page, in the case of mathematical problem solving, also demonstrates that there is an important interaction between the brain, body and environment.

However, in both cases more needs to be said than this to explain how cognition includes manipulations of vehicles external to the skin of the individual.

If I give you an account of the interactions between the brain and the external representations via a more complex version of Webb's analysis of phonotaxis you might well be disappointed, because I will have said nothing of the contents of those representations and I will have said nothing of why the particular manipulations of the representation produce a desired end. In short, I will have told you nothing about why this series of manipulations, as opposed to any others is right, why I *ought* to have done it this way, rather than another. Recognition of this feature of higher cognition should lead us to recognise that we require not only causal explanations of the complex interactions between brain, body and environment, but also normative ones as well.

The normative account of the manipulations of vehicles can be achieved through the work of Peirce and Millikan on representation. We have noted that neither of their accounts of representation is committed to the kind of internalism about representational vehicles that classical cognitive science is. It just does not matter where the mechanisms which produce or consume the representations are located, spatially inside or outside the organism.

We also need to begin to develop an account of how the cognitive capacities of an individual are "sculpted" by the normative interactions with external forms of representation during development. This allows us to claim that the cognitive capacities of an individual extend from the representation rich environment of the individual across the body and brain of that individual (of course, extension here should be seen as being two-way, rather than one-way).

So to return to the question of continuity, we might see the issue as one of mere complexity, where we would need to scale up the explanatory methods that Webb uses to explain phonotaxis, or Brooks's approach to robotics. This has a clear precedent in the case of animate and sensorimotor approaches to perception. But is there something importantly different going on with cognitive practices?

My answer is a qualified yes. Because the manipulations in question involve external representations, often of great complexity, and these representations must be manipulated and consumed in a normative fashion. This normative dimension of cognitive practices is importantly different from the normativity of biological coupling. We will remember that teleonomic representations and teleological representations differ in important respects, because the latter are flexible, context-dependent and open-ended.

However, this is qualified by the argument I have been providing that manipulations of external representations have an evolutionary basis – Mother Nature predisposes us to manipulate external representations. This is highlighted by the examples of teleonomic representation in bees and crickets.

Here is how I propose to resolve this tension concerning cognitive continuity. The human organism is predisposed to manipulate its environmental niche in a variety of ways by its phylogenetic history. The class of manipulation that I have been calling biological coupling provides examples of these kinds of manipulations as adaptations. However, as we saw in the last chapter, the body schemas which govern bodily manipulations of the environment can be fine-tuned through the ontogenetic history of the organism – through learning and training. As with the Vogeltop bowerbird, this tweaking and fine-tuning of a manipulative adaptation is not dependent upon a change in the phylogenetic history of the species, it is a change in the culture of the species. Cultural changes begin, I suggest, as fine-tunings of adaptations, there is, as Tomasello puts it, a cumulative ratcheting effect of these calibrations.

The cognitive evolution of *Homo sapiens* from their hominid forebears gives some idea as to how these fine-tunings of manipulations incrementally developed in a staged way, bringing about genuine alterations to our cognitive capacities. Admitedly some of these changes appear to have been phylogenetic changes, but recent changes appear to be based upon the fine-tuning of adaptations that are cultural.

5.5.1 Hominid evolution

The psychologist Merlin Donald has provided an intriguing account of how exogenous vehicles and cognitive processes might have evolved. Donald (1991) argues that human cognition has evolved across a series of three distinct transitions, each bringing with it its own cognitive advance. Cognitive evolution began with episodic cognition – similar to that possessed by apes – then moved to mimetic cognition – action based and gestural – to mythic cognition – the advent of spoken language – and finally theoretical cognition – involving the evolution of written symbolic languages. The three transitions of cognitive evolution led to changes in the structure of the brain and new communicative and cognitive capacities. The following table indicates the evolutionary timescale involved:

Episodic Culture	3 million years ago
Mimetic Culture	*Homo erectus* 1.5 million years ago
Linguistic Culture	*Homo sapiens* 300,000 years ago
Theoretic Culture	5–10,000 years ago

I will now describe the different properties of each of these stages of cognitive evolution, concentrating most on the development of theoretical cognition.

Episodic cognition is equivalent to that possessed by apes and chimpanzees which originated approximately 3 million years ago. Episodic thought involves the "literal" recall of events, so chimpanzees can recall specific events, but this is their limitation. Whilst apes are sensitive to concrete episodes and have an ability to recall past events, they do not have the kind of abstract symbolic memory of humans (Donald 1991, p. 149). There is nothing more than association going on here, the apes do not have a language with which to label the episodic memories. Language, as we know it, is not yet involved.

With the arrival of *Homo erectus* about 1.5 million years ago, a new cognitive skill evolved. This period of evolution saw "the emergence of the most basic level of human representation, the ability to mime, or re-enact, events" (Donald 1991, p. 16). Donald describes this as "mimesis," or "the ability to produce conscious, self-initiated, representational acts that are intentional but not linguistic" (Donald 1991, p. 168). This ability allowed for cooperation and the social coordination of action (Donald 1991, p. 163). For example, *Homo erectus* developed the ability to follow gaze or indexical pointing and other gestures, which requires the fundamental ability to triangulate, using shared attention, on objects in a shared environment. This communicative ability may also have led to the explosion in tool construction and use. Importantly, these abilities evolve before those required for a spoken language. Donald claims that mimetic cognitive abilities are a necessary pre-adaptation for language (Donald 2001).

The next stage of evolution sees the arrival of language and a "mythic" culture beginning about 300,000 years ago. Donald characterises the function of language in this stage of evolution as being

> evidently tied to the development of integrative thought – to the grand unifying synthesis of formerly disconnected, time-bound snippets of information.... The myth is the prototypical, fundamental, integrative mind tool. It is inherently a modeling device, whose primary level of representation is thematic. The preeminence of myth in early human society is testimony that

> humans were using language for a totally new kind of integrative thought. Therefore, the possibility must be entertained that the primary human adaptation was not language qua language but rather integrative, initially mythical, thought. Modern humans developed language in response to pressure to improve their conceptual apparatus, not vice versa. (Donald 1991, p. 215)

This involved major changes to physiology, psychological organisation, social communication and culture. The emergence of the human speech system allowed for a completely new cognitive capacity for constructing and decoding narrative (Donald 1991).

> Mythic integration was contingent on symbolic invention and on the deployment of a more efficient symbol-making apparatus. The phonological adaptation, with its articulatory buffer memory, provided this. Once the mechanism was in place for developing and rehearsing narrative commentaries on events, and expansion of semantic and propositional memory was inevitable.... At the same time, a major role in attentional control was assumed by the language system. The rehearsal loops of the verbal system allowed a rapid access and self-cueing of memory. Language thus provided a much improved means of conscious, volitional manipulation of the modeling process. (Donald 1991, p. 268)

Mythic culture allows for the transmission of collective knowledge through oral mythology and ritual. Great narratives could be constructed and passed on as tradition.

The third transition leads to theoretic culture, which was achieved only about 5000 years ago with the invention of writing. Writing, in particular, allows the external storage of symbolically represented information. This information now became susceptible to analysis, transformation and intellectual criticism. Human memory is no longer restricted by the boundaries of the body, but is now extended by external memory systems. New cognitive abilities become prevalent. In a mimetic and oral culture rote memorisation is important, this is less important in a theoretical culture where techniques for retrieving and using information stored in external form becomes dominant.

Holding complex forms of information in working memory is now possible by the hybridisation of the working memory space, as constituted, in part, by the external memory field. Donald points to the properties of external symbolic representations, or exograms: they last longer than engrams (biological memories), have greater capacity, are more easily transmissible across media and context and can be retrieved and manipulated by a greater variety of means (1991, pp. 315–6).

The crucial evolutionary movement is from mimetic behaviour to the production of fully external representational systems. The first important step is from purely episodic representation to mimesis. Donald classifies mimetic actions as conscious, self-initiated, representational acts that are intentional but not linguistic (Donald 1991); imitation and re-enactment become behaviours which are iterable (Donald 1991, Rowlands 1999). Rowlands classifies the important features of mimetic behaviour as follows: intentional, being directed at an object; generative, having a "lexicon" of motor actions that are combinable into different forms; public, because exogenous. Mimetic behaviours afford the first real opportunity to share knowledge and skills with each member of a group having to discover it for themselves (Rowlands 1999).

> This transformation from the endogenous representations characteristic of episodic experience to exogenous mimetic representations is the fundamental turning-point in the development of the modern mind. (Rowlands 1999, p. 131)

The development of symbolic representations brings us to the era in which we currently find ourselves.

External written (or printed, or digitised) vehicles offer us something importantly different from biological representations. They allow for storage, different representational formats, and a variety of novel manipulations and transformations. Our cognitive capacities have been both extended and transformed by them.

Therefore, there is a continuity from adapted manipulative abilities (biological coupling) to culturally fine-tuned manipulative abilities on external representations. The crucial transition, as Rowlands and Donald both point out, is from mimesis to language and written vehicles. Once a flexible form of mimetic learning is in place, techniques such as tool making can be easily and cheaply shared amongst members of social groups. New generations do not have to re-discover innovations. Innovations can be passed on through learning and improvements, and refinements of technique can be preserved.

The fine-tuning of manipulative abilities by mimetic learning is once again transformed by linguistic communication, which is a precondition for the development of external representations in a variety of media.

5.6 Conclusion

I have argued that the manipulation thesis and the hybrid mind thesis have a biological basis. The kind of biological coupling found in cases of extended phenotypes shows that natural selection is no respecter of the boundary between organism and environment. Extended phenotypical effects are adaptations and, therefore, the explanation of them is biologically normative. This gets normativity into the picture from the outset. Furthermore, Millikan's biologically normative account of teleonomic representations shows that organisms are biologically disposed to manipulate external representations. There is continuity between cases of biological coupling all the way up to cognitive practices, but at the level of cognitive practices we are dealing with a new kind of representation and a culturally fine-tuned set of manipulative abilities that are governed by norms.

Given these points, I think that we have good reason to suppose that the reciprocal coupling required for all three types of manipulation have a sound biological basis and that even cognitive practices have evolutionary roots. In the next chapter, I shall turn to the formulation of the most important class of manipulation – cognitive practices.

6
Cognitive Practices

> Whence did the wondrous mystic art arise of painting speech
> and speaking to the eyes that we by tracing magic lines are
> taught how to embody and colour thought.
>
> – William Massey

6.1 Introduction

The ideas and arguments of this chapter are the most open to further
investigation, both conceptual and empirical, of any so far broached.
My aim is to provide a framework in which further work could begin
to be done and to show how cognitive practices are dependent upon
the manipulation thesis and hybrid mind thesis, as developed in
the previous two chapters. In both parts of the book, I have been
urging a normative conception of integrated cognitive capacities. The
normative nature of cognition is best illustrated in the class of manipulations I have dubbed cognitive practices.

We have not yet dealt with the cognitive norms by which representational vehicles are manipulated (this will be explained below).
Nor have we dealt with the transformation of our cognitive capacities
by learning the cognitive practices by which such manipulations are
achieved, this will be taken up in the next chapter. This chapter will
focus on cognitive practices and the cognitive norms which govern
the manipulations of external representations.

First of all I shall outline what cognitive norms are, then I shall
look at the great variety of forms of representation and how they are
fitted to cognitive tasks. Then I examine two empirical examples of

cognitive practices and make some suggestions about the future direction of empirical research on cognitive practices. Finally, I provide an integrationist account of linguistic systematicity, demonstrating that the standard internalist account of systematicity is severely lacking. But an account which focuses on the pragmatic and semantic features of external linguistic structures can help explain our systematic linguistic capabilities. This is because linguistic systematicity involves gaining capacities that are constrained and governed by norms of public language, through learning and training.

The arguments of this chapter depend upon the arguments of the previous two chapters. Cognitive practices are dependent upon the manipulation thesis and the hybrid mind thesis, because cognitive practices are abilities to bodily manipulate the environment. The transition from linguistic culture to theoretical culture illustrates that cognitive practices are dependent upon our general linguistic abilities. Our linguistic abilities are enforced by the surrounding linguistic environment, which is structured by linguistic norms. When we learn a language we learn how to participate in this linguistic environment, which includes other language users, we learn how to participate in the creation, maintenance and manipulation of the linguistic environment.

Therefore the discussion of linguistic systematicity illustrates the nature of the normative structure of the linguistic environment and how we come to be able to manipulate it. This discussion indicates how we should go about developing an integrationist account of linguistic capacities and how these capacities involve manipulative abilities that eventuate in cognitive practices. The development of these hybrid manipulative capacities is then explored in the next chapter.

6.2   Cognitive norms

External representations are best understood as representational schemes that are physically embodied, on paper or on a computer monitor for example. What extended mind style arguments have not explained, and what explanations by causal coupling do not show, is how we are able to manipulate a variety of representational types.

There is a great variety of forms of representation which mirrors the great variety of tasks to which we put them. Examples include performing tasks, solving problems, making inferences, planning, working out answers to questions and so on (these are cognitive tasks).

A manipulation of any of these representations is normative, in the sense that we learn or acquire a practice that is an established method of manipulating representations to produce an end. For example, we write down the intermediate stages in problem solving, which can function as part of the working memory space making information available for further manipulation. Or we might directly manipulate the world as part of the problem-solving process, rather than manipulating internal representations. Plans are often written down and then transformed, updated and shared. Lists and diaries allow us to retrieve information from long-term storage and make the information easily and conveniently accessible. The representational properties of maps allow for easy and shared navigation, allowing for the kind of detailed representations and orientations that internal representations cannot provide.

Manipulations of these multifarious representations are all *cognitive practices*. In each case, there is a cognitive task that must be completed. The practice allows us to complete the task by manipulating the representation. The implementation of a cognitive practice depends upon cognitive norms that guide that practice. So, for example, there are

1. *Purposive norms.* The activity is engaged in for a purpose, or end. Cognitive tasks provide these ends.
2. *Corrective norms.* Norms for using representations to correct activity in pursuit of an end. Sutton's instructional nudges are an example of corrective norms at work.
3. *Manipulative norms.* Norms for manipulating inscriptions of a representational system. When we line up numbers to perform a multiplication or division is an example of such a norm in action.
4. *Interpretative norms.* Norms for interpreting inscriptions of a representational system as having some wider significance, not just within the notational system itself but also with regard to the wider world and interests of others. Inscriptions are repeatable representational triads.

There are right and wrong ways to manipulate an external representation to reach a desired end and we learn how to manipulate the representations correctly. An account of cognitive norms has not been sufficiently developed, because the initial focus of cognitive integrationists has been on the causal and constitutive aspects of manipulation. Constitutive in that manipulations constitute cognitive processes and causal because there is a causal interaction between internal and external processing of cognitive vehicles.

We have seen that both body schemas and cultural norms govern our manipulative abilities in Chapter 4. We looked at examples of skill where body schemas give rise to practised movements of the body that are governed by cultural norms. Manipulations of external representations are just another example of body schemas that are governed by norms.

To provide an account of the cognitive norms by which representations are manipulated, we have to look at individual cases of manipulations. For example, cases such as how physicists use diagrams in problem solving or how people use maps to navigate a railway system. Empirical research on these practices, within something like an integrationist framework, is still at an early stage, but it is growing (Hutchins 1995, Cole 1995).

I will begin this process by briefly outlining the nature of normative phenomena and normative explanations. I will then look at the specific case of the cognitive norms required to manipulate mathematical notations, utilising the taxonomy above.

How do we explain normative phenomena? Consider the following brief description of an event:

Thirty people are standing in a field. At each end of the field stand two vertical poles connected by a horizontal pole. An oval object is kicked and then thrown between some of the people in the field, all wearing the same-coloured clothing. Some of the other people, all wearing a colour different from that of the first group, attempt to physically harm the others whilst they are carrying the oval object.

What are they doing? How do we explain their actions? A causal explanation will not be much help and this should be obvious. Instead we need to give a normative explanation, these people are engaging in some kind of conventional practice – they are playing a game of rugby.

There are a variety of types of normative phenomena, for example laws and statutes, conventional practices, maxims, instructions and directives. There are various properties that are associated with these phenomena. The following list is based upon Baker and Hacker (1984, p. 251):

1. they involve some regularity of conduct, at least in principle;
2. our actions are guided by them, they might stipulate that something must or must not be done, they might permit us to do something.
3. or they may stipulate that a particular document, figure or object has a particular role or function;
4. they provide a standard of conduct by which we can be assessed;
5. normative phenomena may originate from an authoritative body or individual, such as a legislative body, or they may arise within a social group as practices and conventions that may be followed and generally accepted, but also subject to critical scrutiny;
6. normative phenomena are general in that they apply to a variety of occasions and be applied by a variety of different people.

The discussion, so far, has focused on social norms – a set of rules widely followed within a community. These rules may be backed by sanctions against those who break them. We should also acknowledge that there is a prescriptive sense of normativity as well, which we can understand by the role of "ought". The prescriptive force of "ought" is most clearly seen in its moral application. However, there are rationally prescriptive oughts – what you ought to do given a relevant set of reasons – and there are socially prescriptive oughts – the "laws" of rugby determine what you ought and ought not to do when playing the game. Similarly, I want to say that there are cognitive oughts – oughts for the correct manipulation of external representations. We should note that the prescriptive force of an "ought" need not depend upon a community's endorsement of it – Kant, for example, would take this to be true of moral "oughts" – however, this issue shall not detain us here.

A prescriptive norm (or "ought") determines what we are required to do in a particular situation, given some relevant principle or rule of conduct. One "ought" not to throw the ball forward in rugby due to law 12 which states,

A throw-forward occurs when a player throws or passes the ball forward. "Forward" means towards the opposing team's dead ball line. (a) Unintentional knock-on or throw-forward. A scrum is awarded at the place of infringement. (b) Intentional knock-on or throw-forward. A player must not intentionally knock the ball forward with hand or arm, nor throw-forward. (International Rugby Board 2005, pp. 73–75)

Following Wedgewood (2002) we can define any concept or principle as normative because of the regulative role it plays in certain practices. Rule 12 of the laws of rugby is normative because it regulates the practice of playing rugby. Therefore principles and concepts that regulate the practice of manipulating external representations are normative. This is the general sense in which I take there to be cognitive norms and must make clear in what sense they regulate cognitive practices. We should note that there are also what Searle (1995) calls constitutive rules which create the possibility of or define an activity. The activity of playing rugby is constituted by acting in accordance with these rules. However, I shall focus on the regulative role of rules, in so far as they are regulative of manipulations.

A central case of a normative manipulation of an external representation, where there is a right and wrong way to do it, is the case of mathematical norms. There are algorithms that we must learn for doing long multiplication and division and there are right and wrong ways of doing long multiplication and division. A clear example of this is the variety of notation systems used in mathematics, such as Venn diagrams, Cartesian graphs, fractions, algebraic formulas, matrices and of course numerals, to name but a few. Importantly, the external vehicles that are manipulated are inscriptions, on paper, blackboard, monitor and so on, of mathematical notations. These inscriptions have a variety of properties that allow them to be manipulated and interpreted (to have significance) in the ways that interest us. The following properties are based upon Dorfler (2002) and Cobb (2002):

The inscriptions of mathematical notations are structured in terms of a spatial arrangement on a page, monitor and so on. The inscriptions can be complex, having parts in which case there will be spatial relationships between these parts. Inscriptions are manipulated in terms of this structure. The inscriptions might be transformed, composed, or combined in various ways according to the relevant manipulative norms.

We are taught manipulative norms for writing down the numbers in this fashion to complete a long multiplication:

343
822

This external notation allows us to perform the simpler set of multiplications starting with 2 times 3. Experts who have well-trained body schemas will be able to fluidly run through the series of operations. Novices will require conscious rehearsal of the manipulative norms for successful completion of the task.

The inscriptions are taken to have some significance, such as a graph that depicts change in some domain. The material inscription is a token of a type, the written numeral 2 stands in this relation to the number 2. There are teleological norms for using general graph representations, such as pie charts, to represent a variety of different quantitative relationships. The representational format is flexible enough to be applied across a range of domains. The representational format can be deployed to meet a variety of cognitive and epistemic ends – it is directible by our purposive norms.

So, there are different cognitive norms available to us. In the mathematical example above, there are norms for manipulating mathematical inscriptions (manipulative norms) and those inscriptions are interpreted as having some kind of significance for some further purpose (interpretative norms). Manipulative norms and interpretative norms apply to manipulations of inscriptions of a representational system. However, there are also norms to use representations, or spoken language, to structure and correct the activities of a cogniser, or cognisers, in a problem-solving task.

In the next section, I go on to describe some of the forms of representation that are manipulated for cognitive purposes.

6.3   Forms of representation

External representations are best understood as inscriptional schemes that are physically embodied, on paper or on a computer monitor for example. It is clear that we use representations in many different ways such as performing tasks, solving problems, making inferences, planning, working out answers to questions and so on. The variety of forms of representation and our use of them to calculate, manipulate and work through problems is as varied as our ends, both practical and epistemic (Peterson 1996, p. 7). The variety of notations can be seen from the following list:

> Algebras, alphabets, animations, architectural drawings, choreographic notations, computer interfaces, computer programming languages, computer models and simulations, diagrams, flow charts graphs, ideograms, knitting patterns, knowledge-representation formalisms, logical formalisms, maps, mathematical formalisms, mechanical models, musical notations, numeral systems, phonetic scripts, punctuation systems, tables and so on. (Peterson 1996, p. 7)

The effectiveness of our abilities to complete cognitive tasks depends to a great extent on the forms of representation we use and the methods we have for manipulating them (Peterson 1996).

The variety of forms of representation is a result of the variety of tasks to which we put them–to our purposive norms (Peterson 1996):

- To draw inferences from the form of representation
- To explore and develop an idea
- Incrementally ticking off items on a shopping list
- To land an aeroplane
- To determine a transport schedule
- To transcribe or re-arrange a piece of music
- To develop a scientific theory with predictive properties.

Specific notations include (Peterson 1996):

- Circuit diagrams developed by an engineer
- A physicist's equations
- The architect's sketch on a sketchpad.

Forms of representation may exist "outside the head", but they are, as Peterson puts it "intra-cognitive", they are part of our cognitive system: "these are external components of a cognitive system with which the internal components interact during a dynamic and task-oriented process of development" (Peterson 1996, p. 8). Removing the external forms of representation would result in the shrinkage of our cognitive systems and knowledge. Undoubtedly, our cognitive capacities for completing cognitive tasks would be severely curtailed.

A manipulation of any of these notations is normative, in the sense that we learn or acquire a practice that is an established method of manipulating notations to produce an end. For example, we learn how to solve problems, we learn how to make plans, we learn how to make lists and use diaries, and we learn how to navigate via maps and so on. These are *cognitive practices*. The practices are cognitive because in each case there is a cognitive task that must be completed. The cognitive practice allows us to complete the cognitive task by manipulating the representation. Hence, the transformation thesis and the cognitive norms thesis taken together are crucial to completing our understanding of the manipulation thesis.

Now we can see why the manipulation thesis is so important. Cognitive practices are a big part of our cognitive lives, we are constantly manipulating external representations to complete many and varied cognitive tasks. We would suffer cognitive shrinkage without the great variety of external representations and we consume and manipulate them in a vast variety of ways. Although none of these cognitive practices are available to us without our mastery over the norms that govern the consumption and manipulation of representational systems.

Take, for example, the practice of recovering belief contents from external vehicles. The contents of beliefs and intentions can be realised in external vehicles such as sentences, lists, plans and agreements (Houghton 1997). The contents of beliefs may be the result of complex calculations and deliberations, and I need to retain that content if I am to be able to do anything with the belief. Take the following example from Houghton (1997, p. 161):

> Say I am decorating a room and need to work out the right amount of paint, wallpaper, carpeting and so on – then I will need to know the dimensions of the room. Once I perform the calculations, using tape measures and so on, I will need to retain the contents of the belief to which my calculations have led me.

So how can I do that? On the one hand, I might try to commit, and might succeed in committing, the details to memory. In which case, it seems, I do indeed internalise the information, the belief-content. On the other hand I might write the information down, making an external record of it. Even if the second strategy utilizes features of the first – for I have to remember that I have made a record and where to find it – these two methods are simply alternative ways of preserving information that has been acquired. (Houghton 1997, p. 161)

Houghton believes it to be perverse to maintain that only if I commit the result of the calculation to internal memory, do I retain the belief. This is because we would have to say that when I commit the result to paper my belief lapses, only for it to be recovered when I later consult the written record. The alternative explanation is more complete and more plausible, that the written result of the calculation is an external representational vehicle from which I can recover the content of my belief and act upon it. Consequently, there are manipulative norms for the storage and retrieval of representational vehicles.

Note that my claim is not that beliefs are external, but rather, that the contents of beliefs are sometimes realised in external representational vehicles and are recoverable from them. This has the distinct advantage of not drawing me into a debate about whether there are belief boxes in the head, whether we should try to give beliefs spatial locations or whether if I store my belief in my diary I am committed to bizarre sounding claims like, I lost my beliefs down the back of the sofa.

In the next section, I outline how some empirical work on how external representations enable us to complete cognitive tasks that would otherwise be very difficult or impossible. The manipulations of external vehicles, in these studies, are distinctly different from internal processes on representations.

6.4 Cognitive tasks and external representations

It is evident that manipulations of external representations enable us to complete some cognitive tasks that we would not otherwise be able to do. To demonstrate this I shall refer to several studies.

Chambers and Reisberg (1985) produced a study that showed that people were better able to access and manipulate drawings than mental images of ambiguous figures such as the duck/rabbit. The study showed that subjects were able to detect ambiguities in external representations of the duck/rabbit, but not in an image recalled to memory. Upon being shown the picture, subjects were asked to form a mental image which they would recall later and then draw. When asked to recall the mental image, they were also asked to provide an alternative interpretation for it by, for example, altering their visual fixation on the image (Clark 2001a, p. 148). Finally, they were asked to draw the image and seek an alternative interpretation of the drawing. Chambers and Reisberg found their results surprising:

> Despite the inclusion of several "high vividness" imagers, none of the 15 subjects tested was able to reconstrue the imaged stimulus. . . . In sharp contrast, all 15 of the subjects were able to find the alternate construal in their own drawings. This makes clear that the subjects did have an adequate memory of the duck/rabbit figure and that they understood our reconstrual task. (Chambers and Reisberg 1985, p. 321)

The subjects were unable to find the interpretation in their "mental image" of the drawing, but they were able to find the interpretation in their drawing. David Kirsh has this to say about the results:

> The implication is that if we want to discover important new elements in a structure, particularly if this requires looking for novel interpretations, we are better off depicting it externally, or consulting some pre-existing external representation of it. *The skills we have developed for dealing with the external world go beyond those we have for dealing with the internal world.* (1995a, p. 64) [my italics]

Further studies (van Leeuwen *et al.* 1999) suggest that the imaginative capacities of the brain are capable of synthetic transformations on images that allow us to combine images into something novel, but that the brain lacks the ability to analytically decompose images into new components (Clark 2001a, p. 149). The evidence suggests that for analytic transformations we need an external representation (a drawing) which, in combination with our perceptual faculties, allows us "...to search the space of analytic transformations" (Clark 2001a, p. 149). Kirsh's interpretation appears sound; our abilities to manipulate external representations take us beyond our bodily internal capacities. However, the integrationist twist is evident in Clark's analysis of the van Leeuwen study. Internal synthetic operations on images work in concert with external operations on drawings via perceptuo-motor loops (reciprocal coupling). Let us look at some further examples of how external representations can transform our cognitive abilities.

Zhang and Norman (1994) argue that external representations produce particular effects on cognition; which they call "the representational effect." "The *representational effect* refers to the phenomenon that different isomorphic representations of a common formal structure can cause dramatically different cognitive behaviours" (1994, p. 88). They cite several cases in point:

- The Arabic numeral system is more efficient for performing multiplication than the Roman numeral system. 73×27 is easier than LXXIII × XXVII. This is the case even though both numeral systems represent the same numbers.
- External rules and representations are used in problem-solving tasks, like the tower of Hanoi problem.

They give examples of external representational types:

external representations are in the world, as physical symbols (e.g., written symbols, beads of abacuses, etc.) or as external rules, constraints, or relations embedded in physical configurations (e.g., spatial relations embedded in physical configurations (e.g., spatial relations of written digits, visual and spatial layouts of diagrams, physical constraints in abacuses, etc.)." (Zhang and Norman 1994, p. 88)

The interesting thing about Zhang and Norman's examples is the recognition of rules and configurations of objects as having a representational function. Clearly the first case of words, sentences and formulae is a standard example of external representations. The more interesting move is to see representational significance in the structure of the environment, as well as rules for manipulating objects in the environment – remember King Beach's mnemonic bar. An example may help us here.

Zhang (2000) provides a different example of external representations as rules embedded in the configuration of objects. An experiment was set up using three isomorphic versions of the tower of Hanoi problem (they are isomorphic, because they embody the same problem, even though they involve different objects). See Figures 1 and 2, for representations of the problem.

The three rules are either memorised, Zhang refers to this as internally represented, or they are externally represented. The rules were not explicitly represented externally but were built into the physical configuration of objects. So, in the orange version, all the rules were memorised. In the donut version (the standard tower of Hanoi problem), rules 1 and 2 were memorised and rule 3 was external. This was because of the physical constraints of the problem. In the coffee version all cups were filled with coffee. Rule 1 was memorised and rules 2 and 3 were external. A smaller cup could not be placed on top of a larger cup – without spillage – and a cup could not be moved if there was another cup on top of it. Zhang's results showed that the more information there was in external representations, the easier the task. The solution times for orange, donut and coffee, were 131.0, 83.0

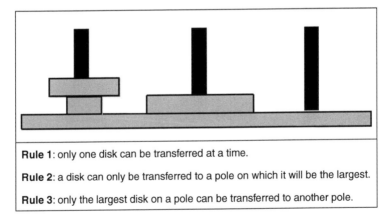

Rule 1: only one disk can be transferred at a time.

Rule 2: a disk can only be transferred to a pole on which it will be the largest.

Rule 3: only the largest disk on a pole can be transferred to another pole.

Figure 1 The Tower of Hanoi problem. The task is to move the three disks from one configuration to another, following the three rules.

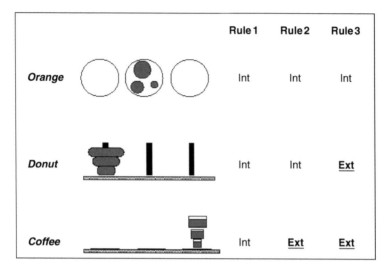

			Rule 1	Rule 2	Rule 3
Orange			Int	Int	Int
Donut			Int	Int	**Ext**
Coffee			Int	**Ext**	**Ext**

Figure 2 Three isomorphs of the Tower of Hanoi problem. See text for explanations.

and 53.9. The solution steps were 19.7, 14.0 and 11.4. The error rates were 1.4, 0.61 and 0.22. If we say that the coffee version was easier because of its external structure, then this is in fact the conclusion we wish to reach.

If we directly interact with the structure of the problem itself, we will find it easier. Zhang and Norman provide the following three reasons for this effect:

- First, external representations provide information that can be directly perceived without being interpreted and formulated explicitly.
- Second, they can anchor cognitive behaviour. That is, the physical structures in external representations constrain the range of possible cognitive actions in the sense that some actions are allowed and others prohibited.
- Third, they change the nature of tasks: tasks with and without external representations are completely different tasks from a task performers' point of view, even if the abstract structures of the task are the same. (Zhang and Norman 1994)

First, we should notice that although Zhang and Norman say that external representations provide information that does not have to be interpreted or explicitly formulated, they are referring to internal representations of the information. In other words, the external representations do not have to be mentally represented before they can be used in cognition.

What Zhang and Norman direct us towards is that the presence of external representations changes the nature of the task at hand, and they allow for direct interaction. Kirsh's notion of an informational space is useful here. The informational space that incorporates representations and other structures in the environment allows us to see manipulations of those representations and structures as cognitive, because such manipulations are taking us closer to our cognitive goals.

This concludes the discussion of cognitive norms and cognitive practices. I turn now to the integrationist account of linguistic systematicity.

6.5 What systematicity is

In the remaining sections of this chapter, I will argue that linguistic systematicity is a hybrid cognitive capacity that involves internal non-classical vehicles and processes and external classical vehicles and processes. In doing so, I will further illustrate the notions of manipulation and hybrid cognitive capacities and I will also begin to link to the transformation thesis and cognitive practices thesis. This is because linguistic systematicity involves gaining capacities that are constrained and governed by norms of public language, through learning and training. This is important, because cognitive practices are highly dependent upon language, for example learning and correction by linguistic channels and the linguistic representation of cognitive norms. If language learning and systematic linguistic capacities were dependent exclusively on internal, and possibly innate, capacities of the individual, some aspects of the account I have been building might seem less plausible, such as the transformation thesis.

Linguistic systematicity involves the capacity to understand and produce the same word in different sentences and to recognise different sentences as having the same grammatical form. The classical explanation of systematic capacities invokes constituently structured representations and processes sensitive to the syntactic properties of those representations. The connectionist solution attempts to produce networks with systematic capacities that do not contain classical representations with constituent structure and processes sensitive to that structure.

The integrationist solution is to take two systems and put them together. The classical system of structured linguistic sentences is an external and autonomous system. The connectionist system of learning algorithms and pattern recognition techniques is coupled to the external linguistic system of spoken and written sentences. The external system provides the forms of grammatical structure and, thereby, the rules by which sentences are structured. This is important if we are to deny that the ability of the network to produce structured sentences must be dependent upon structured representations and processes sensitive to that structure in the head. Rather the network contains processes that are sensitive to structured representations that are *not* in the head.

The integrationist account of systematic capacities should be understood in the context of language acquisition. The child is born into a linguistic environment which guides and sculpts the cognitive profile of the child. We should understand this in terms of the child's becoming a member of a linguistic community. Children are guided by pre-existing linguistic norms, but also by members of the linguistic community who employ those norms, including contextual and pragmatic constraints. Here we can see the link between the transformation and the cognitive practices theses.

Fodor and Pylyshyn motivate systematicity in the following way:

> The easiest way to understand what the systematicity of cognitive capacities amounts to is to focus on the systematicity of language comprehension and production. In fact, the systematicity argument for combinatorial structure in thought exactly recapitulates the traditional structuralist argument for constituent structure in sentences. But we pause to remark upon a point that we'll re-emphasize later; linguistic capacity is a paradigm of systematic cognition, but it's wildly unlikely that it's the only example. On the contrary, there's every reason to believe that systematicity

is a thoroughly pervasive feature of human and infra-human mentation. (Fodor and Pylyshyn 1988, p. 120) (henceforth F&P)

The first thing to notice is that systematicity is motivated by examples of systematic effects in natural language. Secondly there is a claim that thought is generally systematic, so it is not just language comprehension and production that is systematic, but perception and other areas of cognition. This claim is, in part, motivated by the claim that systematicity is pervasive in animal as well as human cognition, again this is a strong claim that requires backing. Unfortunately, F&P do not back up the last claim, they give no arguments or clear examples that would lead us to accept the claim. However, they do have something to say about the move from systematic effects in language to the general systematicity of cognition, and I shall say something about the background assumptions for making this move.

F&P explain the move from the systematicity of language to the systematicity of cognition in the following way:

> What does it mean to say that thought is systematic? Well, just as you don't find people who can understand the sentence "John loves the girl" but not the sentence "the girl loves John", so too you don't find people who can *think the thought* that John loves the girl but can't think the thought that the girl loves John. Indeed, in the case of verbal organisms the systematicity of thought *follows from* the systematicity of language if you assume – as most psychologists do – that understanding a sentence involves entertaining the thought that it expresses; on that assumption nobody *could* understand both the sentences about John and the girl unless he/she were able to think both the thoughts about John and the girl. (Fodor and Pylyshyn 1988, p. 122)

The inference from the systematicity of language to the systematicity of cognition requires the acceptance of a large assumption: that understanding a sentence involves having the thought that it expresses. In their recent paper (Cummins *et al.* 2001) Cummins *et al.*, tell us that Fodor, Pylyshyn and McLaughlin (henceforth FPM) are committed to the following explanation of the systematicity of cognition:

(1) *The representational theory of thought*: having the thought that *P* is having a *P*-expressing mental representation in a certain cognitive role. For example, having a belief *that P* amounts to having a mental representation *that P* in the belief box.

(2) Mental representation is "classical": mental representation has a language like combinatorial syntax and associated semantics.

Putting these two parts together, we get that anyone who can think that *John loves Mary* can think *Mary loves John*, since (i) thinking "Mary loves John" involves tokening a representation of the proposition *that Mary loves John*, and (ii) that representation has constituents corresponding to Mary, John and the relation of loving, which can simply be permuted to yield a representation, and hence a thought, corresponding to the proposition *that John loves Mary*. Fodor, Pylyshyn, and McClaughlin thus conclude that the human system of mental representation must be "classical", that is, a language-like scheme having the familiar kind of combinatorial syntax and associated semantics first introduced by Alfred Tarski. (Cummins *et al.* 2001, p. 169)

This is to explain systematicity by accepting a classical computationalist theory of cognition, such as the language of thought.

Classicists might argue that systematicity implies a classical computational theory of cognition, but we should not just assume that understanding a sentence involves entertaining the thought it expresses, where that thought is classically structured. Indeed Cummins *et al.* go on to say that the characterisation of systematicity given by Fodor *et al.* allows that any theory of cognitive architecture that accounts for our understanding of every sentence will account for systematicity trivially: "if one can understand every sentence, one can understand every systematic variant of any given sentence" (Cummins *et al.* 2001, p. 169). It follows that if connectionism, or indeed any other theory of cognitive architecture, can provide an account of how we understand sentences, it will account for systematicity. So, it might turn out that sentences of language have classical structure, but vehicles of cognition, in the head, do not.

The clearest way to understand linguistic systematicity is through language acquisition. In grammatical development, children go through a "one word stage" between 12 and 18 months, obvious examples being Mama and Dada. However, by the time the child begins to string two words together, 18 months, systematic effects can be observed. A child that can combine a pronoun "my" and a noun "teddy" will have the general capacity to indicate possession – "my Teddy," "my Mummy", "my toy" and so on. The child must have the capacity to string pronouns and nouns together, this involves recognising that a variety of pronouns and nouns can go together. Foss and Hakes (1978) give a list of other capacities learnt at this stage:

1. Naming/noticing: this/that/here + Noun. E.g. "there Teddy," "here kitty."
2. Attribution: Adjective + noun. E.g. "pretty teddy", "naughty teddy."
3. Plurality: Quantifier + noun. E.g. "two cup," "all cars."
4. Actor-action: noun + verb. E.g. "teddy go." Noun + noun. E.g. "Lois (play) baby record." Verb + noun. E.g. "helping Mummy."
5. Requests and imperatives: verb + noun. E.g. "gimme teddy." More/'nother + noun. E.g. "more milk," "nother milk."

The capacities are systematic, because a general grammatical form is acquired to effect a particular linguistic performative. So the verb + noun form can be used to perform a request: "gimme teddy;" obviously a range of verbs and nouns can fill in the roles of the grammatical form, limited only by the vocabulary of the child. The capacity is systematic, because if the child can say "gimme teddy" and knows the word "milk" then the child can say "gimme milk." F&P's simplistic example is anyone who can think that "John loves Mary" can think that "Mary loves John"; or schematically, anyone who can say aRb can say bRa. This is to say that anyone who has the linguistic capacity to produce a sentence with the grammatical form SVO, and who knows the words "Mary", "loves" and "John", will be able to swap the subject and the object nouns of the sentence.

The classical explanation of this capacity is that computational processes combine constituent words to form structured sentences according to grammatical rules. These processes and constituents supervene upon the brain, which is why you find F&P saying:

This bears emphasis because the classical theory is committed not only to there being a system of physically instantiated symbols, but also to the claim that the physical properties onto which the structure of the symbols is mapped *are the very properties that cause the system to behave as it does.* In other words, the physical counterparts of the symbols, and their structural properties, *cause* the system's behaviour. (1988, p. 99)

Connectionists, such as Smolensky, believe that they can explain such systematic capacities, without classical constituents. However, their method is also internalist, because they focus only on "internal" vectorial representations. Given the nature of systematic linguistic capacities, I shall argue that the connectionist can help explain the acquisition of systematic linguistic capacities without needing internal structured representations. This is to give an integrationist account of systematic linguistic capacities.

In the next section, I will question whether systematicity is a ubiquitous property of animal thought, concluding that it is not and that it cannot, therefore, be used to support the claim that human thought is systematic. I then go on to show that a classical computational account of systematic linguistic capacities is hopelessly inadequate in important areas.

6.6   Systematicity in infra-verbal animal thought as evidence for the systematicity of thought

F&P's "John loves the girl" example is supposed to show that there is systematicity in language. Let us assume for the moment that cognition is generally systematic. Why *must* the systematicity of cognition be explained by appeal only to internal cognitive architecture? Why have brains evolved to be intrinsically systematic? One answer to these questions is to say that cognitive architecture is not intrinsically systematic, but language is. Hence, systematic thought is only achievable if one is a language user, in the sense that language confers systematicity on thought. F&P reject this option:

It is not, however, plausible that only the minds of verbal organisms are systematic. Think what it would mean for this to be the case. It would have to be quite usual to find, for example, animals capable of representing the state of affairs aRb, but incapable of representing the state of affairs bRa. Such animals would be, as it were, aRb sighted but bRa blind since, presumably, the representational capacities of its mind affect not just what an organism can think, but also what it can perceive. In consequence, such animals would be unable to learn to respond selectively to bRa situations. (So that, though you could teach the creature to choose the picture with the square larger than the triangle, you couldn't for the life of you teach it to choose the picture with the triangle larger than the square)

It is, to be sure an empirical question whether the cognitive capacities of infraverbal organisms are often structured that way, but we're prepared to bet that they are not. (Fodor and Pylyshyn 1988, pp. 39–40)

This is a strong claim; let us think about what it would entail. Let us for the sake of argument accept that the chimp can have the "thought" that "leopards are dangerous." It does not follow that if he can think about bananas, that he can form the "thought" "bananas are dangerous" (See Sterelny 1990, p. 183, for this example). Dennett makes the same point:

You *do* find organisms – vervet monkeys, for instance – that fail "inference" tests so strangely that although they do not quite past muster as capable of *thinking the thought* . . . that the girl loves John, they do produce evidence of *believing* (in that animal sort of way) that the girl loves John. When that is the sort of state they are in, it is not particularly likely that they are capable as well of being in the state of believing (in the same animal way) that John loves the girl (Cheney and Seyfarth, 1990). There are organisms of which one would say with little hesitation that they think a lion wants to eat them, but where there is no reason at all to think they could "frame the thought" that they want to eat the lion! The sort of systematicity that Fodor and McLaughlin draw our attention to is in fact a pre-eminently language based artefact, not anything one should expect to discover governing the operations in the machine room of cognition. (Dennett 1991, p. 27)

Let us see whether there might be a principled example for systematic animal minds. Ververt monkeys have a repertoire of calls that "alert" the troop to the presence of different predators: leopards, snakes and eagles. These calls eventuate in different avoidance behaviours depending upon the predator call. Let us deal with the issue of the correct interpretation of these calls, do they express a "thought," or "proto-thought"? Following Carstairs-McCarthy (1999, p. 21) we can provide a range of English translations of the vervet eagle call:

1. An eagle!   (NP)
2. There's an eagle overhead!   (declarative sentence)
3. Run from the eagle!   (imperative sentence)
4. Take cover in the bushes!   (imperative sentence)
5. To the bushes!   (prepositional phrase)

We might ask the question, "which of these is best?" As Carstairs-McCarthy notes, this "may seem a silly question" (Carstairs-McCarthy 1999, p. 22). This is because we are being asked to choose between interpretations that differ as to whether the call is declarative or imperative, but this is to choose on the basis of their difference of syntactic status – a declarative sentence, an imperative sentence. There is no obvious sense in which we can do this:

> The trouble is that there is no obvious ground for choosing between them, because the vervet call system (let us call it vervetese) has no syntactic categories and no distinctions of sentence type such as between imperative and indicative. (Carstairs-McCarthy 1999, p. 22)

Although, the vervets have "context-independent" calls for predators, they have no syntax to bring the calls together to form complex strings, sentences in which F&P's systematic effects could occur. Gomez concurs, " . . . call repertoires *a la* vervets are fixed, not productively generated by a lexical or grammatical syntax (Gomez 1998, p. 79). Vervet calls are not compositional, so they cannot display systematic effects. It follows that vervet "thoughts" about predators are not compositional, and therefore not systematic.

Now vervets are good candidates for the kind of organism that should be a systematic thinker, but they are not. So, if systematicity is ubiquitous in infra-verbal organisms, we are owed an account of which organisms these are, because they certainly are not vervets.

Here, at least, are examples of non-systematic animal "thought." It looks likely that we ought to conclude, with Dennett, that the kind of systematicity that F&P are after is the preserve of language using animals like us. In the next section, I shall look at how classical formulations of linguistic systematicity are too simplistic because they focus on the syntactic properties of sentences and ignore their pragmatic and semantic features. These features are important because they place restrictions on the combination of linguistic constituents. These features are pre-eminently features of public language and not an internal language of thought. Therefore, linguistic systematicity is enforced, through learning, by features of external public language and not syntactic properties of the language of thought.

6.7 Grammatical, semantic and pragmatic constraints on linguistic systematic capacities: SVO, poetry and yoda

As we saw in the last section, the examples of "systematicity" used by F&P indicate linguistic capacities to use general grammatical forms, such as SVO, and fill the grammatical roles with a variety of known words. Although this is true, it is not a completely unbounded competence. This is because there are pragmatic, semantic, contextual and grammatical constraints upon the kinds of words that can fill the roles in general grammatical forms. F&P's example is, whoever can say "aRb" can say "bRa". This works fine for simple examples such as "John loves Mary" and "Mary loves John," the subject and object nouns can just be switched. However, this does not follow for all grammatical forms, which superficially appear to have the "aRb," "bRa" structure.

I suggest that there is a problem in F&P's understanding of systematicity and their classical solution. The characterisation of systematicity as the learning of grammatical forms in which a variety of words can occur is accurate. However, the impression that F&P give that all grammatical forms function like the simple "aRb" case is mistaken.

The classical account of systematicity is just the ability to move constituents around to fill different roles in a sentence. However, this does not take into account the following: the position a constituent word occupies in a sentence is dependent upon grammatical form and the meaning of that constituent. We acquire a capacity to produce grammatical and meaningful sentences for some communicative purpose. This is important, because F&P's classical account of systematicity depends upon the syntactic properties of structured representations only – therefore it is at best partial and at worst misleading.

The integrationist account I develop depends upon grammatical rules, pragmatic and semantic constraints, such as communicative purposes, being enforced within the external linguistic system. The problem for the internalist version of the classical approach, and by extension connectionist implementations of it, is that it has no access to these constraints. Given these constraints, not all sentences with the aRb form will be systematic in the classical sense. The following examples illustrate the kinds of constraints that F&P omit, which depend upon the kind of grammatical,[1] pragmatic and contextual knowledge a speaker must develop to produce and understand sentences.

Take these examples of a classic sentence structure that ought to be systematic according to F&P, SVO or generally aRb:

Paul loves Amanda.

Now we are certainly going to want to say that this sentence is classically systematic, because if you can say/understand Paul loves Amanda, you can say/understand Amanda loves Paul. We merely switch the constituent words around, and the sentence retains its meaningfulness. However, let us take the next sentence:

Paul loves fishing.

Is this sentence systematic in the same way as the first? I can say/understand Paul loves fishing so I ought to be able to say/understand fishing loves Paul. But does swapping the constituent words around allow the sentence to remain meaningful? Well, it is not completely nonsensical, but it would be a very odd thing to say and I am not sure precisely what I understand by it. Here is a clearer case:

Paul loves truly.

Whilst it is possible to switch "truly" and "Paul" around, we end up with an ungrammatical sentence. An adverb is incapable of loving someone, the adverb does not play the role of the noun. Other adverbial modifications lead to complete nonsense:

Hang your coat on a hanger (VOA) – Which would amount to: hanger your coat on a hang.

Take the case of sentences of the form aRb, with the relation "is":

Paul is stupid.
Paul is friendly.

Whilst I can switch the constituents to their respective places, the sentences I end up with have an ungrammatical flavour – what thought is being expressed here? What this shows is that it is trivially true that if language is compositional, then one can move constituents around to occupy respective roles in a sentence, but that this often leaves the sentence ungrammatical and sometimes meaningless. The pragmatic, semantic and grammatical constraints on constituent switching are not available to a classical syntax – an internal language of thought.

We are left with the problem that the form aRb does not always have the systematic effect bRa. It is trivially true that we can engage in constituent switching if our purpose is to produce a meaningless or ungrammatical string of words. This is true for the string of words made famous by Chomsky: "Green ideas sleep furiously." Certainly, it is a string of words, but it is neither grammatical nor meaningful. It is not a sentence and it does not express or communicate a thought. Remember that for F&P understanding a sentence involves having the thought it expresses and this amounts to having a classically structured representation tokened in the brain. Hence understanding the sentences "Amanda loves Paul" and "Paul loves Amanda" requires the capacity of the brain to construct those representations from the constituent base. However, the pragmatic, semantic, contextual and grammatical constraints on the formation of thoughts and sentences are not available to the intrinsic capacities of brains. Therefore, the classical approach is partial and often misleading.

What these examples show is that it does not follow that if a sentence has an aRb structure, that we must be able to construct a grammatically and meaningfully correct sentence bRa. Grammatical and pragmatic constraints on sentence construction are not built into the classical account of systematicity. We shall now look at these constraints in more detail. Take the following examples involving verbs:

> (SVA) Paul drinks quickly (again non-systematic except in the trivial sense).
> (SVO) Paul fights Peter (a case of systematicity).
> (SVA) Paul fights aggressively (clearly non-systematic).
> (SVO) Paul drives Pam (systematic).
> (SVA) Paul drives fast (non-systematic).

The SVA forms are all non-systematic in the classical sense because the adverb cannot play the subject role, but clearly the capacity to produce sentences of the form SVA is systematic. If I know the words "Paul", "fights", "aggressively" and "quickly" I can form the sentences: "Paul fights aggressively" and "Paul fights quickly." But this is just to say that the grammatical rules of English determine the legal combinations of words in a sentence. But the classical rules by which constituents get structured into mental sentences are not equivalent to the grammatical rules of English, or French, or Swahili. The classical account of systematicity is not sensitive to the grammatical rules of a particular natural language; therefore, it cannot explain systematic linguistic capacities of English speakers with regard to the grammatical forms that those speakers have mastery of.

The classical examples of systematic sentences all have the form:

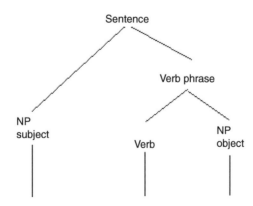

It is clear that the classical characterisation of systematic capacities is inadequate. It is pretty obvious that not all subjects and objects are going to be substitutable and save grammaticality and meaningfulness. The "John loves Mary" example will work as we have seen:

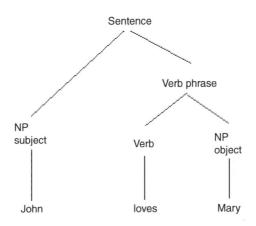

However, take the following example from Chomsky (ironically) (1957, 1965):

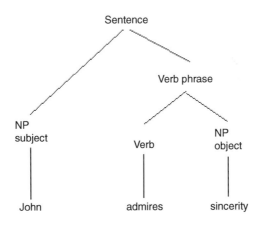

Although the sentence has the SVO structure and John and sincerity are both nouns, "sincerity admires John" is not a systematic variant, it breaches what Chomsky called "selection restrictions." Whilst it is syntactically possible to substitute the noun-phrases in this sentence, it breaches pragmatic and semantic restraints. This demonstrates that systematic capacities have more than just syntactic constraints upon them; systematicity is not merely the ability to shuffle constituents in a sentence. What I acquire, when I acquire a systematic capacity, is the ability to construct certain grammatical forms, like SVO, or SVA, but I do so to construct meaningful sentences for a purpose.[2]

If we take up the themes of the sub-heading of this section, we can see the complexity of the issue. English tends to use the SVO form, Japanese the SOV and Welsh the VSO. Forms other than SVO are used in English to convey emphasis or poetic effect, observe the following (Crystal 1987, p. 98):

VSO govern thou my song (Milton)
OSV strange fits of passion have I known (Wordsworth)
SOV pensive poets painful vigils keep (Pope)
OSV when nine hundred years you reach, look as good you will not
   (Yoda)

If we make Pope into the SVO form we get:

SVO pensive poets keep painful vigils (not very poetic).

Yoda's speech sounds strange to the English ear and this is deliberate, it is for effect. It is close enough to the norm to remain understandable. However, I would not recommend switching to Yoda's OSV from our normal SVO!

Even some of the SVA forms from before work fine in the context of the right sentence: fast drives Paul into the night. The learning of different word order patterns is a complex and often subtle affair and even involves using patterns for particular kinds of effect that cannot be captured by the aRb schema nor by the syntactic properties of the language of thought.

If we focus too hard on syntax we will miss the point here. It seems true that anyone who can think aRb can think bRa and that the ability to understand some sentences is intrinsically connected to the ability to understand others. However, this characterisation of systematicity is just too vague; the examples do not back it up. Contrast the following two sentences where two arguments are related by a predicate: "John *kicked* the ball" and "the Batsman *hit* the ball." John is capable of kicking the ball, but the ball is not capable of kicking John, balls do not kick people.[3] However, the ball is capable of hitting the batsman, so we have two sentences that are syntactically identical, but only in the second case are the noun phrases substitutable. They are not substitutable in the first case, because of the meanings of the verbs and nouns involved.

FPM's classical solution is hopelessly inadequate, because although these two sentences are syntactically identical – they share the same form – the substitutability of the noun phrases is dependent upon semantic and pragmatic constraints, not capturable in purely syntactic terms. The acquisition of systematic capacities requires knowledge of grammatical norms and pragmatic constraints beyond what classicism can offer. The classical interpretation of systematicity just does not scale up.

Two main points arise at this juncture: first, FPM owe us an account of exactly what linguistic systematicity is supposed to be. As things stand, commentators have merely assumed that the aRb structure of some sentences reveals something important about the way that representations must be processed. However, the aRb structure of many sentences does not lead to the systematicity effects of sentences such as "John loves Mary."

The debate between classicists and connectionists has been warped because of the focus on sentences such as the above and not on how systematic linguistic capacities are acquired. The debate does not take into account the recognition and production of grammatical forms according to semantic and pragmatic constraints. In the next section, I look at the classicist claim that constituents must be context-free and whether this explains compositional semantics.

6.8 Compositionality

We have seen that words can function as constituents of sentences, often playing a variety of grammatical roles, such as subject or object. The meaning of a sentence is taken to be dependent upon the meaning of the constituents of the sentence and its syntactic structure, let this stand as a definition of semantic compositionality. As Sainsbury points out (2001, p. 386), it is a truism that *we understand sentences by understanding the words of which they are composed and the arrangement of these words.*

Semantic systematicity involves understanding the contribution a word makes in many different sentences, "Mary loves John", "Fred loves Freda" and so on. The classical explanation of semantic systematicity is that a word makes approximately the same semantic contribution to any expression in which it occurs. According to F&P this makes it a context-free constituent. The classical account of compositionality might explain how the truism holds, but there are many examples which show that a more complex account of compositionality is required. This is because the semantic contribution of a constituent to a sentence will not always be context-free. In these cases understanding the semantic contribution of a constituent will depend upon context and other pragmatic factors.

The following pairs of expressions are not identical in meaning, yet the same constituent appears in each. How do we understand the different contributions made by the same constituent in each expression bearing in mind that context and pragmatics are not allowed in the classical explanation of compositionality?

He *kicked* the ball
The ball *kicked* up off the surface
The *passing* was inaccurate
The boat was *passing* under the bridge
John *arrived* at the airport
John *arrived* at the conclusion
He *fell* to the ground
He *fell* in love
Herodotus gave a *report*
There was a sharp *report*
The *building* took a long time
The *building* collapsed
The *building* on the left was a disaster (Carstairs-McCarthy 1999, p. 25)
He gave the *lecture*
He gave John a *lecture*

The constituents in these examples do not have a context-free meaning which they contribute to each of these sentences; they make a subtly different contribution in each case. Now consider the following cases involving semantic ambiguity, where the meaning of the sentence cannot be determined solely by understanding the words of which they are composed and the arrangement of these words.

> He kept a book
> He went fishing
> He opened up
> He smoked a cigarette (Sainsbury 2001, p. 401)
> He smoked a kipper
> She dropped him
> He was moved

It may be objected that some of these examples rely upon colloquial uses, but of course many utterances and thoughts are full of the colloquial uses of words. In which case, the meaning of the sentence is partly dependent upon contextual and pragmatic factors that are not allowed in the classical approach.

Where does this leave us in the analysis of linguistic systematicity? We have seen that it is unlikely that systematicity is a ubiquitous feature of animal cognition. We have also seen that the classical understanding of systematicity is hopelessly misguided in a large majority of linguistic cases. Most importantly we have argued that systematicity can be best understood within a language-learning context. Children learn grammatical forms of sentences, such as SVO, and that different words can occupy different roles in different sentences. But they also learn that these grammatical forms are used for certain linguistic purposes, and the grammatical and pragmatic constraints place restrictions on the roles that words can play in different sentence forms. These constraints are not available to classicists in their account of systematicity, therefore, their account of systematic linguistic capacities is partial at best.

I have also argued against the classical account of semantic systematicity: that constituent words are context-free because they make the same semantic contribution to each sentence in which they appear. This is the classical way of understanding a principle of compositionality that a sentence is understood in terms of the words of which it is composed and their arrangement. Classical processes are sensitive only to syntactic properties of constituents and these processes compose meaningful sentences only because the syntactic properties mirror the context-free semantics of the constituents.

However, as we have seen, there are many examples of sentences where the constituent words do not make the same semantic contribution. Often, pragmatic and contextual features are required to interpret the sentence as meaning one thing rather than another, but pragmatics and context are not available to classical processes. So, classicism fails to provide an account of how we understand these cases.

The minimal conditions for systematicity are that a child learns different grammatical forms and that words can play a variety of roles within sentences. Connectionists should not feel committed to explaining anything more than this. The alternative possibility is that connectionist systems learn to manipulate grammatical forms, because the linguistic and social environment enforces the grammatical norms during learning. This possibility needs to be taken more seriously.

This alternative can be given as an integrationist account, based on the work of Bechtel (1993, 1997), Bechtel and Abrahamsen (1991), Elman (1991, 1995), Hutchins and Hazlehurst (1995) and Rowlands (1999). I shall show that connectionists do not have to rely on the classical model of language and indeed they ought not to. In sections 6.9 and 6.10, I look at the earliest connectionist attempt at understanding manipulations of structured representations in the environment.

6.9 Preliminary analysis part 1: Real symbol processing

Rumelhart, Smolensky and Hinton give the earliest connectionist account of manipulations of structured representations in the environment in their account of real symbol processing. Their account involves our ability to "manipulate our environment," coupled with connectionist pattern recognition capabilities. Rumelhart, Smolensky and Hinton (1986, p. 44) suggest that there are three cognitive capacities that make us able to do symbol processing:

1. "We are especially good at pattern matching." We "settle" quickly on an interpretation of an input pattern.

2. "We are good at modelling our world." We can "anticipate" the consequences of our actions. Such modelling arises from "internalising our experiences."
3. "We are good at manipulating our environment." "Especially important here is our ability to manipulate the environment so that it comes to represent something."

We should determine what is clear and what is obscure about this. It is clear that connectionist networks (and neural networks in brains) are good at pattern recognition and generalisation. It is unclear what modelling our world is supposed to entail, but if it is internalising our experiences, then this is hopelessly obscure. Fortunately, our ability to manipulate the environment is not obscure, it is certainly true that we manipulate representations in our environment.

The question is, how do connectionists propose to expand these rather vague and general principles into a full-blown account of symbol processing? It seems that the answer lies in the fact that all problem domains can be reduced to a matter of pattern-matching tasks. Experts "see" solutions to problems, where the metaphorical "seeing" should be understood in terms of connectionist pattern matching. Thus chess experts can look at a chess board and "see" the correct move. However, not all problems can be reduced to connectionist-style pattern matching:

> Few if any of us can look at a three digit multiplication problem such as 343 times 822 and see the answer. Solving such problems cannot be done by our pattern matching apparatus, parallel processing alone will not do the trick; we need a kind of serial processing mechanism to solve such a problem. (Rumelhart, Smolensky and Hinton 1986, vol. 2, p. 44)

The serial processing lies in our ability to manipulate the environment. When we write down the numbers in this fashion,

343
822

this external notation allows us to perform the simpler set of multiplications starting with 2 times 3 (as we saw above).

Each cycle of this operation involves first creating a representation through manipulation of the environment, then a processing of this (actual physical) representation by means of our well tuned perceptual apparatus leading to a further modification of this representation. (Rumelhart, Smolensky and Hinton 1986, vol. 2, p. 45)

We have developed external symbol systems to negotiate problem domains where we need to decompose the overall problem into an ordered series of sub-problems in conjunction with internal pattern-matching mechanisms. Let us now turn to an example of a connectionist understanding of how we come to manipulate external logical symbols.

6.10   Preliminary analysis part 2: A connectionist account of logic

Bechtel and Abrahamsen (1991) outline a connectionist approach to learning how to perform logical inferences. The connectionist approach denies that there are already rules of inference in the head, such as modus ponens, which are hard-wired into the brain innately. Rather, we learn rules of inference, such as MP, by being presented with valid and invalid argument forms:

If P then Q   If P then Q
P   Q
∴ Q   ∴ P

Bechtel draws upon his own experience as a teacher of logic in explaining the means by which students learn the rules governing logical forms and their application in arguments (Bechtel and Abrahamsen 1991, p. 165). Students learn by completing exercises as homework, which usually contain a high level of errors at the outset, but improve after the errors have been corrected.

This process of making mistakes and having them corrected seems to be critical to learning informal logic. Moreover, most students do not achieve flawless levels of performance; even on fairly straightforward tests, many students still get 25 percent of the problems wrong. (Bechtel and Abrahamsen 1991, p. 165)

Bechtel contends that students are not just learning abstract rules of deduction, but they are learning how to perform logical inferences, thereby utilising a classic distinction (Ryle 1949). The distinction does not capture everything of interest here though. This is because the students work with valid argument forms which are explicit and external formulations of rules for natural deduction.[4] They constrain and guide the students' construction of arguments. However, as they gain mastery over the rules, they find that they must be sensitive to their application in the correct circumstances. This is a matter of pattern recognition. Bechtel puts the point in the following way:

> At a given step of the proof, there often are rules that are licensed (locally) but do not contribute to the proof (globally). To select an appropriate rule, the student must attend to the larger pattern that is formed by the premises, conclusion, and steps already taken. Although this larger pattern is produced by a serial process (e.g. working backwards from the conclusion), the whole pattern (or parts of it) must be available at each step. It takes a good deal of experience to become aware of these patterns and to become efficient at recognising them. (Bechtel and Abrahamsen 1991, p. 173)

So there is going to be a close and intricate relation between external rules and symbol strings and internal pattern recognition devices – a hybrid solution.

This will give rise to a rather different account of rule-following than a classical one. In a classical account, we expect a symbolic representation of the rule, or an internal systematic process which manipulates mental representations of logical symbols in the head. It is different to this, because the rules are external, the constraints upon the *correct* way to manipulate the external symbols so as to perform a proof are given in the environment and enforced by it. The environment contains the cognitive norms by which external logical symbols are manipulated.

The performance of the proof is dependent upon the recognition of patterns in external logical forms (Rowlands 1999, p. 168) as well as manipulations of those external symbols. It is important that the student gains mastery over this complex process, by recognising logical forms in external symbols and coming to be able to transform those symbols according to the rules for doing so.

Bechtel and Abrahamsen's hybrid account of logical inference does not rely upon internal symbol strings and systematic processes in a language of thought. It involves manipulations of logical notations according to rules of inference and the recognition of patterns of structure in the notations, where particular rules of inference, such as modus ponens, apply. Students come to learn how to use external symbols as tools for reasoning, rather than having those tools built in to a pre-programmed brain. So, connectionists can give an account of "structure sensitive processes" without implementing classical structures internally. The capacity to perform logical inferences also looks to be a systematic capacity, because it requires the recognition of a logical form as a pattern and the recognition that different propositions can play different roles in the inference.

Can we take a similar approach to language learning and, therefore, the acquisition of systematic linguistic capacities? It looks likely given that linguistic systematicity involves recognising grammatical patterns such as SVO and which words can fill which grammatical roles. I shall leave the details of this answer until the next chapter, where it will arise in the context of a Vygotskian theory of psychological development.

6.11   Conclusion

Cognitive integration is founded upon the manipulation thesis. We have seen that a dynamical approach to cognition is required for understanding the four different types of manipulation, because they all involve continuous reciprocal coupling between internal and external components of a greater system. Reciprocal coupling establishes a symmetrical relation between internal processing and external processing, and this differentiates cognitive integration from its asymmetrical externalist cousin. We have also seen the importance of directly manipulating the environment without the need for structured internal representations via sensorimotor contingencies and epistemic actions. This is not a trivial off-loading strategy, but an external component of our processing of a cognitive task.

I have also provided the fundamental conditions for representation and looked at the variety of forms of external representation. But most importantly, we have seen that the normative manipulation of external representations is a crucial part of our completion of higher cognitive tasks. Cognitive practices are governed by cognitive norms. We have seen some ways in which the relevant manipulative capacities are governed by norms, but there is a real need for further empirical work to be done in this area.

Finally, we have seen that linguistic capacities gained through learning and training are another example of manipulative capacity. The integrationist account of linguistic systematicity illustrates the nature of the normative structure of the linguistic environment and how we come to be able to manipulate it. This leads us on to the transformation thesis.

7
Development and the Transformation of Cognitive Abilities

7.1 Introduction

The story so far: I have argued for the manipulation thesis and the hybrid mind thesis. I have also shown that the manipulation of external vehicles requires enforcement by social and cognitive norms (see the previous chapter).

Now we turn to the transformation thesis, which was prefigured in the previous chapter. First we need to establish a developmental framework in which cognitive practices are learned and show that by doing so our cognitive capacities are transformed. This will lead us to an account of the development of cognition in terms of normative interaction with the physical and social environment.

Vygotsky's developmental approach to cognition allows us to understand both how we come to learn and be trained in cognitive practices and how doing so transforms our cognitive capacities.

7.2 The development of cognitive abilities

The focus now turns to how we come to manipulate external representations. We have already looked at examples of the kinds of interaction with the social and physical environments that are required for cognitive integration, but how do we come to interact with our environment in these ways? We shall approach this issue through Vygotsky's approach to psychological development.

Vygotsky was concerned with how the mind is shaped by its cultural and historical context. He took a developmental approach;

we understand the mature mind by looking at its developmental trajectory. These two explanatory approaches help to explain why Vygotsky thought that higher human cognition is shaped by social and environmental interactions (Vygotsky 1981). The Vygotskian approach denies a psychological individualism that would attempt to explain social interaction in terms of individual cognition. Vygotsky provides us with two important explanatory criteria for cognitive integration, which are encapsulated in points 2 and 3 below.

Wertsch (1985, pp. 14–15) identifies three themes that form the core of his theoretical framework:

1. A reliance on a genetic or developmental method.
2. The claim that higher mental processes in the individual have their origin in social processes.
3. The claim that mental processes can be understood only if we understand the tools and representations[1] that mediate them.

We shall take each of these themes in turn, before looking at their consequences for cognitive integration.

As Wertsch points out, genetic here should not be understood in terms of "genes" but as specifying a line of development. Vygotsky and Luria (1930, p. 3):

> Our task was to trace *three basic lines* in the development of behaviour – the evolutionary, historical, and ontogenetic lines – and to show that the behaviour of acculturated humans is the product *of all three lines* of development, to show that behaviour can be understood and explained scientifically only with the help of *three different paths from which the history of human behaviour takes shape.*

We can see that there are evolutionary/phylogenetic forms of human development and that there are historical/cultural forms of human development. Both of these forms of development effect the ontogenetic development of the child. So, we must understand the development of higher human cognition from the perspectives of both the biological evolution of the human species and the historical development of human culture. The effects of these lines of development can be seen in the ontogentetic development of a child's cognitive faculties. We have already been here in Chapter 5, where we looked at the evolution of biological coupling and how epistemic actions and cognitive practices are layered over it.

In each line of development, Vygotsky highlights a point of transition:

> The use and "invention" of tools in humanlike apes crowns the organic development of behaviour in evolution and paves the way for the transition of all development to take place along new paths. It creates *the basic psychological prerequisites for the historical development of behaviour.* Labour and the associated development of human speech and other psychological signs with which primitives attempt to master their behaviour, signify the beginning of the genuine cultural or historical development of behaviour. Finally, in child development, along with processes of organic growth and maturation, a second line of development is clearly distinguished – the cultural growth of behaviour. It is based on the mastery of devices and means of cultural behaviour and thinking. (Vygotsky and Luria 1930, pp. 3–4)

Importantly, each epoch involves a transition to what Wertsch calls a new form of "mediation" (Wertsch 1985, p. 23). In apes it is tool use, in Hominids it was representation use and in child development it is the joint influence of biological development and cultural development. That is to say, that at some point the child's psychological development is governed not just by the biological line of development, but also by the cultural line of development. This involves the development of representation manipulation as part of a representation using community.

It is imperative, however, that we do not assume that development is simply a matter of one or other of the forms of development pointed at by Vygotsky. For example, we might think that the evolutionary/phylogenetic line of development is sufficient because there is a strong motivation for thinking that the use of representations in humans and other species is a product of biological evolution.

As we have seen, there is normativity in the production and consumption of teleonomic representations by bees. Although the normative production and consumption of such representations arises in the biological world, the development of complex teleological representational systems by human cultures is unlikely to be explained in the same way as the normativity of representation production and consumption in bees.

The norms governing human representational systems are of a different nature to the norms governing signs in biological representational systems. This is because of the different range of purposes that representations can have in human sign systems and the wide range of tasks for which they are employed (see the previous chapter). It is unlikely, therefore, that this range of interests and purposes could have been foreseen by evolution. Therefore, we should think of the cultural development of the child as the child's gaining mastery over systems of representation. As we saw in the previous chapter, our manipulations of representations to complete cognitive tasks are regulated by cognitive norms.

Vygotsky's notion of cultural development asks us to think about how biological and cultural lines of development can come together in the child's psychological development. This is not to institute a breach between the two lines of development, but to understand psychological development in terms of interacting developmental "forces." We can understand the interaction of these forces in development, by moving to his analysis of "elementary" and "higher" psychological functions.

7.3   The social development of higher mental processes

From the developmental point of view, higher cognition, for example reasoning and memory, appears first on the "intermental" plane, in other words, in social interaction. Obvious examples would be language learning and joint adult–child problem-solving activities. Cognition, then, is primarily a social phenomenon. However, Vygotsky did claim that higher cognition appears on the "intramental" plane (individual), but only as it is shaped by and derived from intermental cognition. It is crucial, then, to understand how intermental cognition works, for we will be at a loss to understand cognition at the level of the individual. One typical example of this phenomenon is the internalisation of speech.

Piaget labelled the speech that young children engage in when problem solving or engaging in pretend play "egocentric speech." Vygotsky does not view this form of speech as a manifestation of a child's egocentricity, rather, Vygotsky argues (based on empirical studies of infants' speech) that this form of speech is merely the internalisation of speech. It does not disappear with age, it becomes an internal monologue.

The medium via which intermental and intramental cognition are connected is language, it follows that cognition takes place in language. However, other representational artefacts, such as maps, diagrams, charts, mathematical formulae and so on, also mediate it. Vygotsky therefore produces a representational analysis of cognition, we think with representations.

The intermental development of cognition is understood in terms of "the zone of proximal development." The ZPD is the distance between the actual level of development of an individual, what the individual can *actually* do, and the potential level of development, which is what the individual can *potentially do*, with guidance and collaboration from a tutor (the development of systematic linguistic capacities being a case in point). It follows that the individual level of development should not be the exclusive focus of interest. Intermental cognition as mediated through language and interaction with tools and external representations allows us to understand the intramental capabilities of an individual.

Vygotsky's conception of the development of cognition allows us to see the way that language mediates social cognition; and the way in which we interact with external representations allows us to perform higher cognitive acts. We can see this through the example of the development of capacities to manipulate external representations.

7.4 The development of manipulative capacities

Vygotsky denied two claims that dominated twentieth-century psychology, which can be put in the following way: psychology should adopt an explanatory methodology which "begins directly with an object's current features and manifestations" (Vygotsky 1978, p. 62). This is to ignore the developmental study of an object, "its causal dynamical basis" (Vygotsky 1978, p. 62). This is to deny that the mind can be studied without considering its historical development, as well as its development through childhood into adulthood. It is also a denial that there is any one single methodology by which the mind may be studied.

Vygotsky denied that the biological reductionism and behaviourism of his day could give a complete account of the development of cognition. Vygotsky's methodology, by contrast, is to study cognitive development by examining how biological cognitive resources, what he often calls "natural" or "elementary" cognitive functions, are transformed and sculpted by cultural development through manipulations of external representations to produce "higher" cognitive functions. Therefore, it is important to see just how basic biological cognitive resources of the individual interact with the surrounding representational environment.

We can usefully observe Vygotsky putting these points into practice in the following analysis of the co-development of tool use and speech in children. He denies simplistic analyses, current at his time, that assume that the cognitive processes governing tool use and speech are entirely distinct. We can see from the analysis how the development of sign-using abilities in the child begins to alter the way the child engages in problem-solving and other tasks.

7.5   Practical intelligence in animals and children

Vygotsky cites Kohler and Buhler as theorists who compared ape and child behaviour. The important conclusion here is that "the beginnings of practical intelligence in the child (he termed it 'technical thinking'), as well as the actions of the chimpanzee, are independent of speech" (Vygotsky 1978, p. 21). This analogy is mistaken and leads to a false conclusion (technical thinking is divorced from language and concepts) – it perpetuates an old dogma, the distinction between theoria and praxis.

The development of practical intelligence occurs at the same time as the organic development of the child – systematic movement, perception, the brain, hands and so on. "Consequently, the child's system of activity is determined at each specific stage *both by the child's degree of organic development and by his or her degree of mastery in the use of tools*" (Vygotsky 1978, p. 21). "Technical thinking" is taken to be prior to intelligent speech; we enter a chimpanzee-like phase of development, prior to speech. Buhler concludes from his study of the pre-verbal stage of the child's development that

The achievements of the chimpanzee are quite independent of language and in the case of man, even in later life, technical thinking, or thinking in terms of tools, is far less closely bound up with language and concepts than other forms of thinking. (Buhler 1930, pp. 49–51)

Buhler reaches this conclusion, by assuming that the presence of practical/technical intelligence and the absence of speech in a 10-month-old child entails that speech and tool use are separate capacities throughout that child's lifetime (in other words they develop separately).

Vygotsky rejects this simplistic model of child development. Practical intelligence/tool use should not be studied separately from speech/representation use. Before seeing how Vygotsky demonstrates the relation between speech and tool use, we should clarify the argument against such a relation.

Vygotsky reports Kohler's conclusion, on the basis of his experiments with apes, that tool use by apes is independent of any symbolic activity. This conclusion is of course contentious on recent grounds, as reported by Premack and Woodruff (1978). Given the general categorisation of pre-linguistic children as entering an ape-like stage of development, it is no surprise to find Vygotsky reporting that

The study of tool use in isolation from sign use is common in research work on the natural history of practical intellect, and psychologists who studied the development of symbolic processes in the child have followed the same procedure. Consequently, the origin and development of speech, as well as other sign using activity, were treated as independent of the organisation of the child's practical activity. (Vygotsky 1978, p. 23)

In modern parlance, this is equivalent to postulating a speech module which is informationally encapsulated from other modules (those governing practical activity). This assumes, as Vygotsky says, "that the child's mind contains all stages of future intellectual development; they exist in complete form, awaiting the proper moment to emerge" (Vygotsky 1978, p. 24). The use of tools and speech in particular operations holds no interest to psychologists who consider practical activity and sign use to be different avenues of development.

These phenomena are treated as parallel and not interweaving in Piaget's notion of egocentric speech. Vygotsky, though, disagrees.

> Although practical intelligence and sign use can operate independently of each other in young children, the dialectical unity of these systems in the human adult is the very essence of complex human behaviour. Our analysis accords symbolic activity a specific *organizing* function that penetrates the process of tool use and produces fundamentally new forms of behaviour. (Vygotsky 1978, p. 24)

This conclusion should not come as any great surprise to us after the discussion of the manipulation thesis in Chapter 4. Our primary cognitive engagement with the world is bodily, and body schemas underlie our capacities for cognitive manipulations, as well as manipulations that are non-cognitive. During the learning and training of a skill, such as a shot in tennis or cricket, we are guided by norms. Even in these cases symbolic activity can have an organising function. Body schemas are governed by norms, the norms have an organising function which results in new sensorimotor programmes.

7.6   Social interaction and the transformation of practical activity

The mistake is to think that practical activity and speech develop in entirely different ways and in entirely different circumstances. One way to reach this conclusion is to compare neonate behaviour with the behaviour of apes and conclude that neonates go through an ape-like stage. Apes do not naturally begin to manipulate external representations. Since neonates are comparable to apes, they also do not engage in representation using activities. A further extension of the conclusion is to say that practical intelligence and representation use are independent in adults.

Vygotsky's position is entirely different. The onset of speech restructures practical activity. In the sense that it produces new relations to the environment and organises behaviour in a way that Vygotsky labels, "uniquely human." In cases where the child must act in such a way as to bring about a goal, the activity is accompanied by egocentric speech.

The following examples incorporate the feedback structure of coupled dynamics and exhibit the purposeful, normative and self-corrective aspects of problem solving. The examples make clear the importance of Vygotsky for understanding how the child's higher cognitive functions are formed through mastery of cognitive practices. As the child gains mastery of cognitive practices, she gains access to self-controlled behaviour, which helps her to complete cognitive tasks such as problem solving.

Vygotsky cites an experiment where a child's speech arises spontaneously in a problem-solving situation. The speech is continuous throughout the experiment as observed.

Levina's experiments posed problems to 4- and 5-year olds, such as obtaining candy/sweets from a cupboard. The candy was placed out of reach so that the child could not reach it directly. Vygotsky describes the concurrent roles of speech and action (including tool use) in the child in the following way:

> As the child got more and more involved in trying to obtain the candy, "egocentric" speech began to manifest itself as part of her active striving. At first this speech consisted of a description and analysis of the situation, but it gradually took on the "planful" character, reflecting possible paths to a solution of the problem. Finally it was included as part of the solution. (Vygotsky 1978, p. 25)

A four-and-a-half-year-old girl was asked to get candy from a cupboard with a stool and a stick as tools. The experiment was described by Levina in the following way (his descriptions are in parentheses, the girls speech is in quotation marks):

> (Stands on a stool, quietly looking, feeling along a shelf with stick). "On the stool." (Glances at experimenter. Puts stick in other hand) "Is that really the candy?" (Hesitates) "I can get it from that other stool, stand and get it." (Gets second stool) "No that doesn't get it. I could use the stick." (Takes stick, knocks at the candy) "It will move now." (knocks candy) "It moved, I couldn't get it with the stool, but the, but the stick worked."

Vygotsky claims that activity is not just accompanied by speech in children, but that speech plays a specific role in such activity. He claims that the experiments show two important facts:

1. A child's speech is as important as the role of action in attaining the goal. Children not only speak about what they are doing; their speech and action are part of *one and the same complex psychological function*, directed toward the solution of the problem at hand.
2. The more complex the action demanded by the situation and the less direct its solution, the greater the importance played by speech in the operation as a whole. Sometimes speech becomes of such vital importance that, if not permitted to use it, young children cannot accomplish the given task." (Vygotsky 1978, p. 26)

There may be a stage of development in the pre-linguistic infant that is analogous to apes, but to focus on this at the expense of later developmental stages is disastrous. In the example, the child is structuring the task space *in* speech. We can see that this distinguishes the actions of the speaking child from those of the ape. It does so because it gives the child greater freedom in her approach to the problem. The child's options are not determined by a direct link between herself and the goal. The child engages in a series of preliminary activities. These acts are mediated, in the sense that they do not *directly* achieve the goal, rather, they change the structure of the problem such that the goal can be achieved. This should remind us of epistemic actions. The actions are part of the cognition, the structuring of the problem, there is a complex interaction between speech, action and perceptual processes (amongst others). Furthermore, the child uses speech as a corrective tool, "that didn't work, so I'll try this." Speech as corrective tool is normative in this case, because it is a medium through which the child can correct her activity in the process of achieving the desired result. So, the norms here are not static propositional rules that are learnt and rigidly followed at all.

Vygotsky considers these actions to be mediated by speech or representations in general. These representations function as stimuli, but are not restricted by the current visual field of the child. Planning in speech allows for a broader range of actions. This demonstrates the integration of speech, perception and action in the child. However, actions that specifically alter the way the task can be solved are mediated by representations. It is a mistake to think that actions are always directly related to their goals. Many actions make achieving a goal easier, without directly achieving the goal itself – an epistemic action.

The child's actions are not a series of random movements in the hope of achieving the goal. Speech allows for planning and the mediation of actions. However, why should this worry the internalist? After all, is not this egocentric speech just a result of internal processes?

The answer is no and to see why we must turn to one of Vygotsky's most famous claims. Vygotsky makes the claim forcibly in the following quote:

> It is necessary that everything internal in higher forms [of psychological processes] was external, that is, for others it was what it now is for oneself. Any higher mental function necessarily goes through an external stage in its development because it is initially a social function. This is the centre of the whole problem of internal and external behaviour . . . When we speak of a process, "external" means "social." Any higher mental function was external because it was social at some point before becoming an internal, truly mental function." (Vygotsky 1981, p. 162)

This is the transformational component of cognitive integration. The development of the cognitive capacities of an individual are sculpted by the cognitive norms in the social environment of that individual. It makes higher cognition possible, because it gives the individual mastery over the cognitive norms by which external representations are manipulated by the individual. Vygotsky expresses this in the claim that children "master the rules in accordance with which external signs must be used" (Vygotsky 1981, pp. 184–5).

He gives the following example of how such mastery may be achieved:

> At first the indicatory gesture is simply an unsuccessful grasping movement directed at an object and designating a forthcoming action. The child tries to grasp an object that is too far away. The child's hands, reaching toward the object, stop and hover in mid air. . . . Here we have a child's movements that do nothing more than objectively indicate an object.

When the mother comes to the aid of the child and comprehends the movement as an indicator, the situation changes in an essential way. The indicatory gesture becomes a gesture for others. In response to the child's unsuccessful grasping movement, a response emerges not on the part of the object, but on the part of another human. Thus, other people introduce the primary sense into this unsuccessful grasping movement. And only afterwards, owing to the fact they already have connected the unsuccessful grasping movement with the whole objective situation, do children themselves begin to use the movement as an indication. The functions of the movement itself have undergone a change here:

> from a movement directed toward an object it has become a movement directed toward another human being. The grasping is converted into an indication . . . this movement does not become a gesture for oneself except by first being an indication, that is, functioning objectively as an indication and gesture for others, being comprehended and understood by surrounding people as an indicator. Thus the child is the last to become conscious of the gesture. (Vygotsky 1981, pp. 160–1)

The child's behaviour is shaped by the normative environment in which she acts. Gesturing becomes indicating once it is interpreted as being so by another, thus the child is brought into the practice of a social norm – this is an example of the transition from prelinguistic to indicational stages of linguistic development. It is in this way that the higher cognitive capacities of the individual are sculpted, by interactions with the social/representational environment.

There is further evidence for the development of the ability to manipulate external representations which has had a recent corroboration. Children are capable of distinguishing representational types at an early age and before they have gained mastery over their use. In conjunction with an adult they are capable of performing simple uses of notations to complete cognitive tasks, such as remembering words. The experiments indicate that children learn, through interaction with an adult/teacher, that cognitive tasks can be completed by cognitive practices. According to Vygotsky:

> The following can serve as examples of psychological tools and their complex systems: language; various systems for counting; mnemonic techniques; algebraic symbol systems; works of art; writing; schemes, diagrams, maps, and mechanical drawings; all sorts of conventional signs; and so on. (Vygotsky 1981, p. 137)

Vygotsky refers to experiments by Luria on the development of writing skills in children:

> In his experiments children who were as yet unable to write were confronted with the task of making some simple form of notation. The children were told to remember a certain number of phrases that greatly exceeded their natural memory capacity. When each child became convinced that he would not be able to remember them all, he was given a sheet of paper and asked to mark down or record the words presented in some fashion. (Vygotsky 1978, p. 114)

The children were often "bewildered" by the suggestion because they could not yet write. The experimenter gave the children examples of pencil-marks they could make and showed them how they could be used as symbols for recalling the corresponding phrases. In the case of 3–4-year-old children, they ignored the paper when attempting recall of the phrases. However, there were cases where children used the paper and pencil marks in a remarkable way:

> In these cases, the child also makes meaningless and undifferentiated squiggles and lines, but when he reproduces phrases it seems as though he is reading them; he refers to certain specific marks and can repeatedly indicate, without error, which marks denote which phrase. An entirely new relationship to these marks and a self-reinforcing motor activity arise: for the first time the marks become mnemotechnic symbols. (Vygotsky 1978, p. 115)

The children placed individual marks on different parts of the page allowing the child to associate different marks with different phrases. A mark in one corner of the page would be used to recall "cow," another further up to recall "chimney-sweep" and so on. The techniques used by the children are early forms of indicatory notations used for memory purposes. Children learn early and quickly how to use external notations for cognitive purposes. Once they master the techniques of writing and drawing a wide range of cognitive practices become available to them.

In more recent times, Annette Karmiloff-Smith (1992) has conducted similar experiments and reached similar conclusions to

Vygotsky and Luria. Preliterate and predrawing children were asked to "draw" a dog and "write" its name. The children naturally objected that they could not draw or write, they were encouraged to pretend to be doing so. The distinctions between the pretend drawings and the pretend writings were marked, this indicates that even at a very young age toddlers distinguish between different representational types, even though they have not yet learnt to master them. Furthermore, the children indicated the distinction between scribbles as drawings, "that's a dog" and wiggly horizontal lines as writing, "and that says Fido" (Karmiloff-Smith 1992, p. 143). The ability of young children to flexibly grasp the distinct roles of representational forms is quite remarkable, especially considering that they do not yet have mastery over them. It illustrates something important about the child's developing psychological capacities, they rapidly develop manipulative abilities in conjunction with cognitive norms and learn to deploy them to complete cognitive tasks. In the previous chapter, I outlined the cognitive norms that children acquire through development such that they become proficient at completing cognitive tasks by becoming proficient in cognitive practices.

Having outlined the developmental trajectory of the child's cognitive capacities, we should now return to the issue of the development of systematic linguistic capacities.

7.7 Connectionist language learning without internal structured representations

The connectionist approach to language learning based upon powerful pattern recognition abilities can be connected up with the linguistic and normative structure of the environment in explaining the development of systematic linguistic abilities. The main connectionist approach to language learning, I will analyse, is based upon Elman's recurrent networks. Elman developed a recurrent network which could predict subsequent words in a sequence of simple English sentences (Elman 1990). He also developed a recurrent network that could classify words according to their lexical category, such as verb or noun and recognise grammatical structures such as subject–verb number agreement (Elman 1991).

The networks are designed so as to exploit the temporal structure of spoken English, as sequences of words. Importantly, the grammatical and semantic function of words in a sentence is dependent upon prior and subsequent words. Standard feed-forward networks have a problem with input that is sequentially structured over time, because once the network begins a cycle of processing input, it begins all over again with a new input. Therefore, the network can have no "memory" of the previous input, when it is processing that new input.

A recurrent network has an extra layer of units, called context units, which are connected to the hidden layer of units. The context units copy the activation values distributed over units of the hidden layer, the context units then feed that activation pattern back to the hidden layer on the next cycle of processing. The hidden units receive both new input from the input layer and the copy of the activation values on the hidden units, of the previous cycle, from the context layer.

However, the network will fail quite badly if it is exposed to sentences of random complexity in the training set. Elman discovered that the best way to deal with this problem was to phase the training, to train the network on batches of sentences beginning with the simplest structure, working up to those with the most complex structure. This phasing of the training works along side a phasing of the memory, by only allowing the context units to become active in stages during the training.

Giving the net a limited memory in the early phases of training limits its access to the most complex sentences in the training set. The net is constrained to sentences four or five words long. This allows the net to be exposed to sentences with verb-subject-number agreement structure, but not complex embeddings and long distance dependencies in the early stages of training (Clark 1993, p. 141). Latterly, the net with full memory can deal with sentences of full complexity. The network "grows" as it learns, Elman explains the benefits in the following way:

> Seen in this light the early limitations on memory capacity assume a more positive character. It is natural to believe that the more capacityful a network, the greater its ability to learn a complex domain. However this appears not always to be the case. If the domain is of sufficient complexity, and if there are abundant "false solutions," then the opportunities for failure are great. What is

required is some way to artificially constrain the solution space to just that region which contains the true solution. The initial memory limitations fill this role; they act as a filter on the input, and focus learning on just that subset of facts which lay the foundations for future success. (Elman 1991, p. 8)

Before we analyse this phased approach to learning, I want to look at whether Elman's net is relying upon internal structured representations. Elman's net identified words that conformed to grammatical principles, such as plural verbs following plural subjects (Bechtel 1997, p. 17), but how did it achieve high degrees of accuracy? The network does not have a memory containing representations of whole sentences that it maps onto input. With each new input, the activation pattern from the previous cycle is carried over to the context units, as we have seen. Again, the patterns stored by the context units are not explicit representations of sentences, as Bechtel puts it:

> Recurrent connections allow the network only to keep a constantly degrading trace of some aspects of previous cycles (which aspects it retains depends upon the task the network is required to learn). (Bechtel 1997, p. 17)

When Elman (1991) performed a principal component analysis on the network, he found that the hidden units retained information about a particular grammatical function, such as a subject–verb agreement, where this information will be used later.

However, Bechtel suggests (1997, p. 18) that this indicates that the hidden layer of the network stores these activation patterns only until they are no longer needed, at which point the network loses them. The recurrent network does not store concatenatively or functionally (in Van Gelder's sense) compositional representations of sentence structure. The hidden layer retains information about previous input patterns, but the patterns on the hidden layers are not merely representations of the structure of input sentences. The activations on the hidden unit layer encode information about how to produce particular grammatical forms. It does not follow from this that the hidden layer must store representations that have classical constituent structure:

Even when the items with which they are working (in this case word sequences) are syntactically structured, they do not need to build up a complete representation of that structure. They may need to represent some information about that structure (for example, that a subject for which a verb has not yet been encountered is singular), but this is done on a need-to-know basis. In the case of language, then, what is represented (actual discourse) will be syntactically structured, but the mental or network representation need not be. (Bechtel 1997, 18)

The network has the capacity to recognise particular grammatical forms, without producing internal representations that share the structure of those forms. Let us return to the phased approach to learning. Are there any principles behind the "phased" approach to learning other than expediency?

This issue is best approached from a developmental perspective, because we can better see how there would be a need for phased memory and phased training. Both the phased structure of learning and memory appear to have a grounding in the constraints on children during language learning. Whilst Elman's "toy" model clearly does not model the stages that children go through in language learning, there are principled reasons for thinking that children go through a phased process of language acquisition. Secondly, although children are exposed to the full complexity of language from the first stages of development, they are not sensitive to the full complexities in the early stages.

The two points of interest here are that we will find a phased learning and a phased memory within the child's process of acquiring language. What we will also find is the important role of the linguistic environment, in terms of providing the forms of grammatical structure and, thereby, the rules by which sentences are structured. This is important, if we are to deny that the ability of the child to produce structured sentences must be dependent upon structured representations and processes sensitive to that structure in the head. Let us deal with point one first.

Mark Rowlands (1999) provides an account of the phased nature of language acquisition, based upon recent research in developmental psychology and linguistics. He puts forward four phases in the following way:

1. *Prelinguistic.* This phase is essentially constituted by interactions between child and caretaker made up of face-to-face and back-and-forth vocalisations. Such vocalisations are not linguistic as such and there is no expectation that they should meet the formal requirements of the language community (Snow 1977).
2. *Indicational.* To possess an indicational capacity is to possess the ability to draw the attention of another to some aspect of the environment. In this phase, the child is increasingly treated as a language user. The caretaker and other interlocutors begin to modify their phrasing and other aspects of speech in relation to the child, and the child, in turn, exhibits a developing skill of articulation (Reed 1995).
3. *Transitional.* This phase represents the child's entrance into the surrounding linguistic community. This entrance seems to be driven by two central factors, one environmental, one internal, both of which strongly reinforce each other. First, during indicational language use, the child eventually acquires special lexemes that serve, in the linguistic community, as argument-structuring devices (Tomasello 1992). Secondly, the transitional language user undergoes considerable cognitive development which enables her to better understand environmental structures and relationships which are of fundamental importance in learning how to predicate (Pinker 1984, Gopnik and Meltzoff 1993).
4. *Predicational.* In this phase, the child is a fully-fledged member of the linguistic community, having mastered the practice of predication and in virtue of this, being able to use language in a generative, systematic, and inferentially coherent way.

Each phase in the sequence is a necessary condition for the next and there is a natural progression from an earlier phase to the next phase. Rowlands points out that once the learner has successfully negotiated one phase they are moved straight into the next (Rowlands 1999, p. 192). This is a more realistic description of the phased nature of language acquisition, than the phased training of the Elman net.

What we see here is the child coming to acquire ever more complex capacities, but that the having of these capacities and the exercising of them is not a wholly internalist affair. The child must come to mastery over the structure of ever more complex linguistic forms, but this depends upon the ability to recognise and use the structure available in the environment (what is usually called "the input"). Alongside this, the phased nature of the Elman net, along with its pattern-recognising capabilities, allows us to see how structure-sensitive processing is possible without all the processing and structure being in the head.

This brings us to point 2. The moral of the phased learning case is that the environment guides and sculpts the cognitive profile of the child. We should understand this in terms of the child's becoming a member of a linguistic community. Children are guided by pre-existing linguistic norms, but also by members of the linguistic community who employ those norms. This can be understood in terms of Vygotsky's notion of "the zone of proximal development which is: The distance between the actual level of development of an individual, what the individual can *actually* do, and the potential level of development, which is what the individual can *potentially* do with guidance and collaboration from a tutor." The individual level of development should not be the exclusive focus of interest. If we consider the child, or net, on its own, with input just as sentences in a given language, we will miss the complex structure of the linguistic environment and the child's interaction with it. We will also miss the role of the caretaker/tutor who interacts with the child and provides linguistic input and guidance.

This is a more promising approach to systematicity than either classicism, or connectionism when narrowly construed. The integrationist approach allows for the recognition and production of grammatical forms alongside a sensitivity to contextual and pragmatic factors, whilst focusing on whether or not internal representations are constituently structured does not.

The integrationist gives due respect to the role of the environment and rejects an internalist analysis of the causal capacities of nets as dependent only upon intrinsic causal properties of those nets. Structure-sensitive processing is dependent upon the structure explicitly available in the environment. The linguistic environment plays an ineliminable role to the processing of sentences; the net is not self-contained with respect to it.

This is a properly hybrid explanation of systematic linguistic capacities. Pattern-recognition processes of connectionist networks and the external structures and rules for their use are fully integrated and we can think of this integration in terms of embodied and embedded connectionist networks.

Imagine, following Hurley (1998, Ch. 10; 2001), a neural network that has become attuned to its linguistic environment by sensory – motor interactions. The network, sensory-motor feedback loops and linguistic environment, including speech and written text, constitute an integrated dynamical system. The linguistic structure in the environment when coupled to the network constitutes an important component of the system, negating the need for isomorphically structured representations to be stored in the network's memory.

To give a full account of cognitive integration, we will need to explain the interaction between network and linguistic environment in terms of dynamical feedback loops. We will also need to explain the network's developmental trajectory by the way it is sculpted and guided by the grammatical and pragmatic norms enforced by the linguistic environment. Together this gives us an account of the development of the manipulative abilities of the embodied and embedded network. This, I suggest, is the future of connectionist research on how we acquire systematic capacities in language learning.

Given the minimal conditions for systematicity that a child learns different grammatical forms and that words can play a variety of roles within sentences, we can see that some connectionist approaches to language learning are promising. The classicist attempt to explain systematicity was shown to be wanting in the previous chapter, primarily because of its focus on constituent swapping and neglect of pragmatic and contextual features of natural languages. Importantly, this leads us to the conclusion that systematicity is not a causal property that *must* supervene on the brain. Thus, we are free to give a rival account of structure-sensitive processing that depends upon relational properties, as well as intrinsic properties. As a result, we have an example of a hybrid approach to cognition.

7.8 Conclusion

Vygotsky provides a framework in which the transformation thesis can be understood. We can see how higher cognition is developed through interaction with an environment containing structured representational systems. The individual must gain mastery over these representational systems, allowing for the kinds of coupled processes described by the cognitive integrationist. Gaining mastery over representations involves gaining mastery over their normative application.

Vygotsky shows us how it is possible to bring together the normative and causal aspects of cognitive integration, by showing us the social development of higher cognitive processes. We can see this most clearly in the account of the co-development of practical activity and speech. The example of the child restructuring the task space in speech and implementing changes to the environment through action to achieve a desired goal illustrates this perfectly. Vygotsky allows us to see the necessarily social dimension to the study of cognition, which is how we can begin to understand the normative dimension of the study of cognition.

Conclusion: Cognitive Webs

What would we be without our cognitive webs? Like the spider, we create, maintain and manipulate our cognitive webs. Unlike the spider, we also share these webs and learn how to fine-tune them in all sorts of ways. There are webs that are primarily iconic and linguistic ones that are primarily symbolic, and although the webs help us achieve cognitive ends, there are many different ends and many different ways in which the webs allow us to achieve them.

"What do you think about humans and their cognitive webs?" Having read this book, I'd like to hear your answer.

Notes

1 Cognitivism and internalism

1. And I do not for one minute think that this chapter will do sufficient shaking to disabuse philosophers of their cherished metaphysical assumptions.
2. We do not find scientists in general doing this in fact, is there a mark of the chemical that chemists must first delineate? Or a mark of the physical for physicists?
3. Some cognitive scientists work with dynamical systems whose processes and vehicles are different again as we shall see in the next chapter.
4. This is what Kirsh and Maglio (1994) call a pragmatic action, rather than an epistemic action – see Chapter 5.
5. Why I think this only becomes clear when we distinguish between pragmatic actions and cognitive practices as types of manipulation. In principle my manipulation of the calculator could be a pragmatic action, but it is not a cognitive practice.
6. Considered pluralistically, this could be non-classical computation in neural networks, or classical computation on symbolic representations.
7. Fodor uses the term "causal power," but I shall be using the term "causal capacity" instead, otherwise nothing is changed in the argument.
8. A wide property is one that involves an objects relations to its local environment or the history of the object.
9. Wilson disagrees with Fodor on this point (Wilson 1995, p. 33), he does not think that individuation by sameness of causal properties is the same as individuation by causal capacities, this is because, "The concept of a causal property is broader than the concept of a causal [capacity]: [capacities] are essentially forward looking in a way that properties in general are not. The relevant causal similarities between two phenomena in a given discipline may involve the *causes* of those phenomena or the causal relations they stand in, rather than what those phenomena are capable of causing" (Wilson 1995, p. 33).
10. I shall take a narrow/intrinsic property to be a current, internal, physical property. I shall take a wide/relational property to be dependent upon some object, or objects, other than the object that has the property; or if historical, then dependent upon some time prior to the present.
11. The biological function of A is to contract the muscles in the presence of predators, but once it has acquired this function it can be activated by the presence of things other than predators. This is not a statistical matter; the neuron may fire more often when there are no predators near, but its adapted function is to fire when predators are near. Hardly any sperm fertilize an ovum, yet this is their function.

12. This condition is weaker than the formality condition, because external vehicles are manipulated in virtue of their formal and semantic properties, computers do not directly manipulate vehicles in virtue of their semantic properties because they do not understand them, humans do.
13. Wilson's wide computationalism (1995, 2004) is simply the hypothesis that computational systems include subjects plus parts of their embedding environments and has close affinities with Clark's extended mind and Rowland's environmentalism.

2 Externalism, dynamics and the extended mind

1. This is indeed the strategy that Clark takes up in Memento's Revenge (Clark 2007).
2. Or indeed, writing with pens and paper, different tools that enable the process of writing.
3. Extended mind theorists are still developing a clear sense of what external vehicles are. Sometimes they talk of external vehicles as affordances (Hurley 1998, Rowlands 1999), sometimes tools such as pen and paper (Clark and Chalmers 1998) and sometimes inscriptions such as written sentences, diagrams and other notations. This ambiguity needs to be eliminated, especially as some criticisms of the extended mind focus on the claim that artefacts and tools can play the role of external vehicles.
4. But embodied in external media – such as notebooks, computer screens and so on. This relates to the worry expressed in the previous footnote, that artefacts are vehicles of cognition. On my reading, inscriptions of sentences and symbols are cognitive vehicles. The notebook is the *medium* in which the vehicles are realised, rather than the vehicle itself.

3 Defending cognitive integration

1. I do not endorse this way of thinking. It is just a natural conclusion to be drawn if A&A pursue the strong version of the stipulation.
2. Fodor's argument that only a rational psychology is tractable, from Chapter 1, is a direct ancestor of this claim – thanks to John Sutton for pointing this out.
3. Thanks to Tim Bayne for pointing this out to me.

4 Cognitive integration: Embodied engagements and the manipulation thesis

1. If cricket is not your game, much of what Sutton says is equally applicable to a baseball batter or a tennis player. If sport is not your thing at all, then imagine the same kind of dynamics required for an open skill such as dancing.

2. The kinds of situational factors include the type of bowler, fast or slow, the direction in which the ball is heading after pitching – towards the batsman or away from the batsman – the placement of the fielders and the nature of the pitch – some pitches reward quicker bowling and some slower bowling. In baseball the relevant features might include the difference between a fastball and a curve ball.

3. This is another example of how even explanations of how bodies work will require a wide explanation and not the narrow explanation favoured by the internalist.

4. It might be that some internal representations result from the completion of an epistemic action.

5. Even a cleaned-up version of the parity principle will do no more than provide intuitive support for the extended mind.

6. I shall assume that K&M's talk of mental computation is equivalent to our talk of cognitive processes.

7. Hence turning on the TV by manipulating the remote is a pragmatic action.

8. The Peircean principle is based upon and is an updating of the incredibly important work on sign action, or representation in use, of the pragmatist philosopher Charles Sanders Peirce. Unfortunately his writing is not very accessible, and it is rather spread out amongst the vast corpus of his work that remained unpublished during his lifetime. Nevertheless, his work has been a core influence on Millikan's biosemantics, Von Eckardt (1993) and O'Brien and Opie (2004). But more importantly, it seems to me, he has got a far more accurate and detailed account of the conditions for representation than anyone else.

9. To avoid tedious repetition of the word representation(al), I shall use vehicle, salience and consumer as shorthand.

5   The evolution of the hybrid mind

1. One immediate response may be, if a nest is considered to be part of the bird's "organismic system," because it is essential to survival, then so is oxygen, and oxygen is not part of the bird's organismic system in the same way that its wings are. The simple answer is that oxygen is not a feature of an organism which has been selected for as an adaptation, rather an organism's lungs – or other oxygen filtering system – is an adaptation to an environment containing oxygen. I shall return to this later.

2. Trivially, the characteristics of an aquatic niche will be distinct from those of a desert.

3. Especially by Gould and Lewontin, 1979, and Varela, Thompson and Rosch (1991).

4. We might ask the "why?" question, "why does the flying fish fall back into the water?" The answer will be partly to do with gravity and partly to do with the physical structure of the fish. This is not an adaptive

question, if we were to try to answer the question, "why does the flying fish leap out of the water?" And gave a purely physical answer, we would still be left puzzled. The question can only be answered in terms of the function's "purpose", an adaptive answer.

5. This is just the distinction between genotypes, collections of genes and phenotypes, the effects of those genes. Proper functions of devices are selected for over time, because the genes which specify them as phenotypic effects are selected for over time.

6 Cognitive practices

1. Of a particular natural language such as English or Swahili, not a universal *lingua mentis*.
2. Of course, on rare occasions I might deliberately produce ungrammatical, or nonsensical sentences in the context of a nonsense poem, or humour. But I hardly think these rare instances constitute the norm. Without the norm, they would not have the desired effect.
3. Notice that the ball could *kick* up off the pitch, but again the meaning of *kick* here is dependent upon context.
4. Compare with Norman and Zhang's work on external rules and representations above.

7 Development and the transformation of cognitive abilities

1. Where Vygotsky uses the term "sign" throughout this chapter, I shall understand it in the sense of representation I have been using throughout in accord with the Peircean principle. Vygotsky provides his own triadic account of signs and psychological processes.

Bibliography

Adams, F. and Aizawa, K. (2001). The bounds of cognition. *Philosophical Psychology*, 14, 43–64.

Adams, F. and Aizawa, K. (2007). Defending the bounds of cognition. In Richard Menary (ed.), *The Extended Mind*. Aldershot: Ashgate.

Avital, E. and Jablonka, E. (2000). *Animal Traditions: Behavioural Inheritance in Evolution*. Cambridge: CUP.

Ballard, D.H. (1991). Animate vision. *Artificial Intelligence Journal*, 48, 57–86.

Baddeley, A.D. (2000). Short-term and working memory. In E. Tulving and F.I.M. Craik (eds), *The Oxford Handbook of Memory*. New York: OUP. pp. 77–92.

Baker, G.P. and Hacker, P.M.S. (1984). *Language, Sense and Nonsense*. Oxford: Blackwell.

Beach, K. (1988). The role of external mnemonic symbols in acquiring an occupation. In M.M. Gruneberg and R.N. Sykes (eds), *Practical Aspects of Memory*. New York: Wiley, 1, 342–6.

Bechtel, W. (1993). What knowledge must be in the head in order to acquire language. In B. Velichkovsky and D.M. Rumbaugh (eds), *Communicating Meaning: The Evolution and Development of Langauge*. Hillsdale, NJ: Lawrence Erlbaum Associates.

Bechtel, W. (1997). Embodied Connectionism. In D. Johnson and C.E. Erneling (eds), *The Future of the Cognitive Revolution*. Oxford: Oxford University Press. pp. 187–208.

Bechtel, W. and Abrahamsen, A. (1991). *Connectionism and the Mind*. MA: Blackwell.

Beer, R. (1995). Computational and dynamical languages for autonomous agents. In R. Port and T. van Gelder (eds), *Mind As Motion Dynamics, Behavior and Cognition*. Cambridge, MA: MIT Press. pp. 121–48.

Bodén, M. and Niklasson, L. (1996). Features of distributed representations for tree-structures: A study of RAAM. In *Current Trends in Connectionism – Proceedings of the 1995 Swedish Conference on Connectionism*, Skövde, Lawrence Erlbaum.

Brooks, R.A. (1991). Intelligence without representation. *Artificial Intelligence*, 47, 139–159.

Buhler, K. (1930). *Mental Development*. New York: Harcourt, Brace.

Burge, T. (1986). Individualism and psychology. *The Philosophical Review*, 94(1), 3–45.

Carstairs-McCarthy, A. (1999). *The Origins of Complex Language: An Inquiry into the Evolutionary Beginnings of Sentences, Syllables, and Truth*. Oxford: OUP.

Chambers, D. and Reisberg, D. (1985). Can mental images be ambiguous? *Journal of Experimental Psychology: Human Perception and Performance*, II(3), 317–28.

Chalmers, D. (1990). Syntactic transformations on distributed representations. *Connection Science*, 2, 53–62.

Cheney, D.L. and Seyfarth, R.M. (1990). *How Monkeys See the World: Inside the Mind of Another Species*. Chicago: University of Chicago Press.

Chomsky, N. (1957). *Syntactic Structures*. The Hague: Mouton.

Chomsky, N. (1965). *Aspects of the Theory of Syntax*. Cambridge: The MIT Press.

Churchland, P.M. and Churchland, P.S. (1983). Stalking the wild epistemic engine. *Nous*, 17, 5–18.

Churchland, P.S., Ramachandran, V. and Sejnowski, T. (1994). A critique of pure vision. In C. Koch and J. Davis (eds), *Large Scale Neuronal Theories of The Brain*. Cambridge, MA: MIT Press.

Churchland, P.S. and Sejnowski, T. (1992). *The Computational Brain*. Cambridge, MA: MIT Press.

Clark, A. (1989). *Microcognition: Philosophy, Cognitive Science and Parallel Distributed Processing*. Cambridge, MA: MIT Press.

Clark, A. (1993). *Associative Engines: Philosophy, Cognitive Science and Parallel Distributed Processing*. Cambridge, MA: MIT Press.

Clark, A. (1997). *Being There: Philosophy, Cognitive Science and Parallel Distributed Processing*. Cambridge, MA: MIT Press.

Clark, A. (1999). Where brain, body, and world collide. *Journal of Cognitive Systems Research*, 1, 1, 5–17.

Clark, A. (2000a). A case where access implies qualia? *Analysis*, 60(1), 30–8.

Clark, A. (2000b). Phenomenal immediacy and the doors of sensation, *Journal of Consciousness Studies*, 7(4), 21–4.

Clark, A. (2001a). *Mindware*. Oxford: OUP Press.

Clark, A. (2001b). Reasons, robots and the extended mind. *Mind and Language*, 16 (2), 121–45.

Clark, A. (2001c). *Mindware: An Introduction to The Philosophy of Cognitive Science*. New York and Oxford: OUP.

Clark, A. (2003). *Natural Born Cyborgs: Minds, Technologies and the Future of Human Intelligence*. New York: Oxford University Press.

Clark, A. (2005). Intrinsic content, active memory and the extended mind. *Analysis*, 65, 1–11.

Clark, A. (2006). Material symbols. *Philosophical Psychology*, 19(3), 1–17.

Clark, A. (2007). Memento's revenge: The extended mind extended. In Richard Menary (ed.), *The Extended Mind*. Aldershot: Ashgate.

Clark, A. and Chalmers, D. (1998). The extended mind. *Analysis*, 58, 7–19.

Cobb, P. (2002). Reasoning with tools and inscriptions. *Journal of The Learning Sciences*, 11, 187–215.

Cole, M. (1995). *Cultural Psychology: A Once and Future Discipline*. Cambridge: Harvard University Press.

Crystal, D. (1987). *Cambridge Encyclopedia of Language*. Cambridge: CUP.

Cummins, R. and Schwartz, G. (1987). Radical connectionism. In T. Horgan and J. Tienson (eds), *The Southern Journal of Philosophy (Proceedings of the Spindel Conference, Memphis State University)*, Supp. vol. XXVI, 43–62.

Cummins, R., Blackmon, I., Byrd, D., Poirer, P., Roth, M. and Schwartz, G. (2001). Systematicity and the cognition of structured domains. *Journal of Philosophy*, 98, 167–85.

Dartnall, T. (2005). Does the world leak into the mind? Active Externalism, "Internalism" and Epistemology. *Cognitive Science*, 29, 135–43.

Dawkins, R. (1976). *The Selfish Gene*. Oxford: OUP.

Dawkins, R. (1982). *The Extended Phenotype*. Oxford: OUP.

Dennett, D. (1987). *The Intentional Stance*. MA: MIT Press.

Dennett, D. (1990). The myth of original intentionality. In K.A. Mohyeldin Said, W.H. Newton-Smith, R. Viale and K.V. Wilkes (eds), *Modeling the Mind*. Oxford: Oxford University Press. pp. 43–62.

Dennett, D. (1991). *Consciousness Explained*. London: Penguin.

Devitt, M. (1990). A narrow representational theory of mind. In W. Lycan (ed.), *Mind and Cognition: A Reader*. Oxford: Blackwell.

Dewey, J. (1929). *Experience and Nature* (revised edition). New York: Dover, 1958.

Dretske, F. (1988). *Explaining Behavior*. Cambridge: MIT.

Dreyfus, H.L. and Dreyfus, S.E. (1986). *Mind over Machine: The Power of Human Intuition and Expertise in the Era of the Computer*. Oxford: Blackwell.

Donald, M. (1991). *Origins of The Modern Mind*. Harvard: HUP.

Donald, M. (2001). *A Mind So Rare: The Evolution of Human Consciousness*. New York: W.W. Norton.

Dorfler, W. (2002). *Instances of Diagrammatic Reasoning*. Unpublished MS.

Edelman, G. (1992). *Bright Air, Brilliant Fire*. London: Penguin.

Egan, F. (1991). Must psychology be individualistic? *Philosophical Review*, 100, 179–203.

Egan, F. (1992). Individualism, computation, and perceptual content. *Mind*, 101, 443–59.

Elman, J. (1990). Finding structure in time. *Cognitive Science*, 14, 179–211.

Elman, J. (1991). Distributed representations, simple recurrent networks and grammatical structure. *Machine Learning*, 7, 195–225.

Elman, J. (1995). Language as a dynamical system. In R.F. Port and T. van Gelder (eds), *Mind as Motion*. MA: MIT Press.

Elman, J., Bates, E.A., Johnson, M., Karmiloff-Smith, A., Parisi, D. and Plunkett, K. (1996). *Rethinking Innateness: A Connectionist Perspective on Development*. Cambridge, MA: MIT Press.

Fodor, J. (1980). Methodological solipsism considered as a research strategy in *Cognitive Psychology*. Reprinted in D.M. Rosenthal (ed.), *The Nature of Mind*. 1991, Oxford: OUP.

Fodor, J. (1987). *Psychosemantics*. MA: MIT Press.

Fodor, J. (1990). *A Theory of Content and Other Essay*. Cambridge MA: MIT Press.

Fodor, J. (1997). Connectionism and the problem of systematicity (continued): why Smolensky's solution still doesn't work. *Cognition*, 62(1), 109–19.

Fodor, J. and Pylyshyn, Z. (1988). Connectionism and cognitive architecture. *Cognition*, 28(1–2), 3–71.

Fodor, J. and McClaughlin, B. (1990). Connectionism and the problem of systematicity; why Smolensky's solution doesn't work. *Cognition*, 35, 183–204.

Fogassi, L., Gallese, V., Fadiga, L., Luppino, G., Matelli, M. and Rizzolatti, G. (1996). Coding of peripersonal space in inferior premotor cortex (area F4). *J. Neurophysiology*, 76, 141–57.

Foss, D.J. and Hakes, D.T. (1978). *Psycholinguistics: An Introduction to the Psychology of Language*. New Jersey: Prentice-Hall.

Gallagher, S. (2005). *How the Body Shapes The Mind*. Oxford: OUP.

Gallie, W.B. (1952). *Peirce and Pragmatism*. London: Penguin Books.

Gibson, J.J. (1979). *The Ecological Approach to Visual Perception*. Boston: Houghton Mifflin.

Godfrey-Smith, P. (1996). *Complexity and The Function of Mind in Nature*. Cambridge: CUP.

Gomez, J. (1998). Some thoughts about the evolution of LADS, with special reference to TOM and SAM. In P. Carruthers and J. Boucher (eds), *Language and Thought*. Cambridge: CUP, pp. 76–93.

Gopnik, A. and Meltzoff, A.N. (1993). Words and thoughts in infancy: The specificity hypothesis and the development of categorization and naming. In C. Reeve-Collier and L. Lipsitt (eds), *Advances in Infancy Research*. Norwood: Ablex.

Gould, S.J. and Lewontin, R.C. (1979). The Spandrels of San Marco and The Panglossian Paradigm: A critique of the adaptationist programme. *Proceedings of The Royal Society of London*, Series B, 205 (1161), 581–98.

Graziano, M.S.A. and Gross, C.G. (1994). Mapping space with neurons. *Curr. Dir. in Psych. Scio.*, 3, 164–7.

Graziano, M.S.A. and Gross, C.G. (1998). Visual responses with and without fixation: Neurons in Premotor cortex encode spatial locations independently of eye position. *Exp. Brain Res.*, 118, 373–380.

Houghton, D. (1997). Mental content and external representations. *The Philosophical Quarterly*, 47(187), 159–77.

Hurley, S. (1998). *Consciousness In Action*. Cambridge MA: Harvard Press.

Hurley, S. (2001). Perception and action: Alternative views. *Synthese*, 129, 3–40.

Hunt, G.R. (1996). Manufacture and use of hook-tools by New Caledonian Crows. *Nature*, 379, 249–51.

Hutchins, E. (1995). *Cognition In The Wild*. Cambridge, MA: MIT Press.

Hutchins, E. and Hazlehurst, B. (1995). How to invent a lexicon: The development of shared symbols in interaction. In G.N. Gilbert and R. Conte (eds), *Artificial Societies: The Computer Simulation of Social Life*. London: UCL Press.

Hutto, D. (1999). *The Presence of Mind*. Amsterdam: John Benjamins.

International Rugby Board (2005). *The Laws of The Game*. Dublin: IRB.

Karmiloff-Smith, A. (1992). *Beyond Modularity: A Developmental Perspective on Cognitive Science*. Cambridge MA: MIT Press.

Kirsh, D. (1995a). The intelligent use of space. *Artificial Intelligence*, 73, 31–68.

Kirsh, D. (1995b). Complementary strategies: Why we use our hands when we think. In Johanna D. Moore and Jill Fain Lehman (eds), *Proceedings of the Seventeenth Annual Conference of the Cognitive Science Society* Hillsdale, NJ: Erlbaum. pp. 212–17.

Kirsh, D. and Maglio, P. (1994). On distinguishing epistemic from pragmatic actions. *Cognitive Science*, 18, 513–49.

Lewontin, R. C. (1979). Sociobiology as an adaptationist program. *Behavioral Science*, 24(1), 5–14.

Lewontin, R. C. (1982). Organism and environment. In H. Plotkin (ed.), *Learning Development and Culture: Essays in Evolutionary Epistemology*. New York: Wiley.

Lewontin, R. C. (1983). The organism as the subject and the object of evolution. In R. Levins and R. Lewontin (eds), *The Dialectical Biologist*. MA: HUP. pp. 85–106.

Liszka, J. (1996). *A General Introduction to The Semeiotic of Charles Sanders Pierce*. Bloomington: Indiana University Press.

Macdonald, C. (1995). Introduction: Classicism vs connectionism. In C. Macdonald and G. Macdonald (eds), *Connectionism: Debates on Psychological Explanation*. Oxford: Blackwell.

McClelland, J., Rumelhart, D. and the PDP Research Group (eds) (1986). *Parallel Distributed Processing: Explorations in The Microstructure of Cognition*. Vols I and II Cambridge, MA: MIT Press/Bradford Books.

McGinn, C. (1989). *Mental Content*. Oxford: Blackwell.

Menary, R. (2006a). Attacking the bounds of cognition. *Philosophical Psychology*, 19, 329–344.

Menary, R. (2006b). What is radical enactivism? In R. Menary (ed.), *Radical Enactivism*. Amsterdam: John Benjamins.

Menary, R. (2007a). Writing as thinking. *Language Sciences*, 29.

Menary, R. (2007b). The extended mind and cognitive integration. In R. Menary (ed.), *The Extended Mind*. Aldershot: Ashgate.

Mendola, J. (2003). A dilemma for asymmetric dependence. *Nous*, 37(2), 232–57.

Millikan, R. (1984). *Language, Thought, and Other Biological Categories*. Bradford Books/MIT Press.

Millikan, R. (1993). *White Queen Psychology and Other Essays for Alice*. Bradford Books/MIT Press.

Millikan, R. (2002). *The Varieties of Meaning: The Jean-Nicod lectures*. Cambridge: MIT Press.

Myin, E. and O'Regan, J.K. (2002). Perceptual consciousness, access to modality and skill theories. *Journal of Consciousness Studies*, 9(1), 27–46 (20).

Neander, K. (1995). Misrepresenting and malfunctioning. *Philosophical Studies*, 79, 109–41.

Neisser, U. (1976). *Cognition and Reality: Principles and Implications of Cognitive Psychology*. San Francisco: W.H. Freeman.

Neisser, U. (1981). John Dean's memory: A case study. *Cognition*, 9, 1–22.

Noë, A. (2004). *Action in Perception*. Cambridge: MIT Press.

O'Brien, G. and Opie, J. (2004). Notes towards a structuralist theory of mental representation. In H. Clapin, P. Staines and P. Slezak (eds), *Representation in Mind: New Approaches to Mental Representation*. New York: Elsevier.

O'Regan, J.K. and Noë, A. (2001). A sensorimotor account of vision and visual consciousness. *Behavioral and Brain Sciences*, 24(5), 939–1011.

Peirce, C.S. (1931). *Collected Paper of Charles sanders Peirce*, eight volumes, eds Hartshorne, C., Weiss, P. and Burks, A. Cambridge MA: Harvard 1931–60 (vol./paragraph).

Peterson, D. (1996). *Forms of Representation*. Bristol: Intellect Books.

Pinker, S. (1984). *Language Learning and Language Development*. Cambridge: HUP.

Pinker, S. (1997). *How the Mind Works*. New York: W.W. Norton & Company.

Port, R. and van Gelder, T. (1995). *Mind As Motion: Dynamics, Behavior and Cognition*. Cambridge, MA: MIT Press.

Premack, D. and Woodruff, G. (1978). Does the chimpanzee have a theory of mind? *Behavioral and Brain Sciences*, 1, 515–26.

Putnam, H. (1975). *Mind, Language, and Reality*. Cambridge: CUP.

Putnam, H. (1981). *Reason Truth and History*. Cambridge: CUP.

Reed, E. (1995). The ecological approach to language development: A radical solution to Chomsky's and Quine's problems. *Language and Communication*, 15(1), 1–29.

Rosenfield, I. (1989). *The Invention of Memory*. New York: Basic Books.

Rowlands, M. (1997). Teleological semantics. *Mind*, 106(422), 279–303.

Rowlands, M. (1999). *The Body in Mind: Understanding Cognitive Processes*. Cambridge: CUP.

Rowlands, M. (2003). *Externalism*. Chesham: Acumen.

Rumelhart, D.E., Smolensky, P. and Hinton, G.E. (1986). Schemata and sequential thought processes in PDP models. In J. McClelland and D. Rumelhart (eds), *Parallel Distributed Processing: Explorations in the Microstructure of Cognition*, vol. 2, Cambridge: M.I.T. Press, p. 44.

Rupert, R. (2004). Challenges to the hypothesis of extended cognition. *Journal of Philosophy*, 101, 389–428.

Rupert, R. (2007). Representation in extended cognitive systems: Does the scaffolding of language extend the mind? In R. Menary (ed.), *The Extended Mind*. Aldershot: Ashgate.

Ryle, G. (1949). *The Concept of Mind*. London: Penguin.

Sainsbury, M. (2001). Two ways to smoke a cigarette. *Ratio*, 14, 386–406.

Segal, G. (1989). Seeing what is not there. *Philosophical Review*, 98, 189–214.

Segal, G. (1991). Defence of a reasonable individualism. *Mind*, C(40), 485–494.

Searle, John (1995). *The Construction of Social Reality*. New York: The Free Press.

Smolensky, P. (1988). On the proper treatment of connectionism. Reprinted in C. Macdonald and G. Macdonald (eds), *Connectionism: Debates on Psychological Explanation*. Oxford: Blackwell. pp. 28–89.

Smolensky, P. (1995). Constituent structure and explanation in an integrated connectionist/symbolic cognitive architecture. In C. Macdonald and G. Macdonald (eds), *Connectionism: Debates on Psychological Explanation*. Oxford: Blackwell. pp. 223–290.

Snow, C. (1977). The development of conversation between mothers and babies. *Journal of Child Language*, 4, 1–22.

Stalnaker, R. (1989). On what's in the head. Reprinted in D. Rosenthal (ed.), *The Nature of Mind*. Oxford: OUP. pp. 576–89.

Stich, S. (1983). *From Folk Psychology to Cognitive Science: The Case Against Belief*. Cambridge: MIT Press.

Sterelny, K. (1990). *The Representational Theory of Mind*. Oxford: Blackwell.

Sterelny, K. (2003). *Thought in a Thostile World: The Evolution of Human Cognition.* Oxford: Blackwell.

Sutton, J. (2007). Exograms and Interdisciplinarity: History, the extended mind, and the civilizing process. In Richard Menary (ed.), *The Extended Mind.* Aldershot: Ashgate.

Thelen, E. and Smith, L. (1994). *A Dynamic Systems Approach To the Development of Cognition and Action.* Cambridge, MA: MIT Press.

Tomasello, M. (1992). *First Verbs: A Case Study in Early Grammatical Development.* New York: CUP.

Van Gelder, T. (1990). Compositionality: A Connectionist Variation on a Classical Theme. *Cognitive Science,* 14, 355–384.

Van Gelder, T. (1991). What is the "D" in "PDP"? An overview of the concept of distribution. In S. Stich, D. Rumelhart and W. Ramsey (eds), *Philosophy and Connectionist Theory.* Hillsdale N.J.: Lawrence Erlbaum Associates.

Van Leeuwen, C., Verstijnen, I. M. and Hekkert, P. (1999). Common unconscious dynamics underlie uncommon conscious effects: A case study in the interactive nature of perception and creation. In J.S. Jordan (ed.), *Modelling Consciousness across the Disciplines.* Lanhan, MD: University Press of America.

Varela, F., Thompson, E. and Rosch, E. (1991). *The Embodied Mind.* MA: MIT Press.

Vogel, S. (1981). Behavior and the physical world of an animal. In P. Bateson and P. Klopfer (eds), *Perspectives in Ethology,* 4.

Vygotsky, L. (1978). *Mind In Society.* Cambridge MA: Harvard Press.

Vygotsky, L. (1981). The instrumental method in psychology. In J. Wertsch (ed.), *The Concept of Activity in Soviet Psychology.* Armonk, NY: Sharpe.

Vygotsky, L. and Luria, A. (1930) (1993). *Studies on the History of Behavior. Ape, Primitive, and Child.* Hillsdale, NJ: Erlbaum. (Original work published 1930.)

Waskan, J. and Bechtel, W. (1997). Directions in connectionist research: tractable computations without syntactically structured representations. *Metaphilosophy,* 28, 31–62.

Webb, B. (1994). Robotic Experiments in Cricket Phonotaxis. Cliff, David, Husbands, Philip, Meyer, Jean-Arcady, and Wilson, Stewart W. *From Animals to Animats 3: Proceedings of the Third International Conference on the Simulation of Adaptive Behaviour.* MA: MIT Press. pp. 45–54.

Wedgewood, R. (2002). The aim of belief. *Philosophical Perspectives,* 16, 267–97.

Weir, A., Chappell, J. and Racelnik, A. (2002). Shaping of hooks in New Caledonian Crows. *Science,* 297, 981.

Wertsch, J. (1985). *Vygotsky and The Social Formation of Mind.* MA: HUP.

Wheeler, M. (1996). From robots to Rothleo: The bringing forth of worlds. In M. Boden (ed.), *The Philosophy of Artificial Life.* Oxford: OUP, pp. 209–36.

Wheeler, M. (2005). *Reconstructing The Cognitive World: The Next Step.* MA: MIT Press.

Wheeler, M. and Clark, A. (1999). Genic representation: Reconciling content and causal complexity. *British Journal for the Philosophy of Science,* 50(1), 103–35.

Wilson, R.A. (1995). *Cartesian Psychology and Physical Minds: Individualism and the Sciences of the Mind.* Cambridge Studies in Philosophy. Cambridge: CUP.

Wilson, R.A. (2004). *Boundaries of the Mind: The Individual in the Fragile Sciences – Cognition.* Cambridge: CUP.

Wittgenstein, Ludwig (1953). *Philosophical Investigations.* MA: Blackwell.

Yarbus, A. (1967). Eye movements during perception of complex objects. In L.A. Riggs (ed.), *Eye Movements and Vision.* New York: Plenum Press. pp. 171–196.

Zhang, J. and Norman, D.A. (1994). Representations in distributed cognitive tasks. *Cognitive Science,* 18, 87–122.

Zhang, J. and The Coordination of External representations. (2001). Internal mental representations in display-based cognitive tasks. In *Lecture Notes in Computer Science: Theory and Application of Diagrams: First International Conference, Diagrams 2000, Edinburgh, Scotland, UK, September 2000, Proceedings.* Berlin/Heidelberg: Springer, 72–128.

Index